LITERATURE MADE EASY

ARTHUR MILLER'S

THE CRUCIBLE

Written by LONA McGREGOR
WITH TONY BUZAN

BARRON'S

CONTENTS

There are five important things you must know about your brain and memory to revolutionize
the way you study:

- ◆ how your memory
  ("recall") works *while* you are learning
- ◆ how your memory works *after* you have finished learning
- ◆ how to use Mind Maps – a special technique for helping you with all aspects of your studies
- ◆ how to increase your reading speed
- ◆ how to prepare for tests and exams.

Recall during learning
– THE NEED FOR BREAKS

When you are studying, your memory
can concentrate, understand, and
remember well for between 20 and 45
minutes at a time, then it needs a break.
If you carry on for longer than this
without a break, your memory starts to
break down. If you study for hours nonstop, you will remember
only a small fraction of what you have been trying to learn, and
you will have wasted hours of valuable time.

So, ideally, *study for less than an hour*, then take a five- to ten-
minute break. During the break listen to music, go for a walk, do
some exercise, or just daydream. (Daydreaming is a necessary
brain-power booster – geniuses do it regularly.) During the break
your brain will be sorting out what it has been learning, and you
will go back to your books with the new information safely
stored and organized in your memory banks. We recommend
breaks at regular intervals as you work through the Literature
Guides. Make sure you take them!

Recall after learning

— THE WAVES OF YOUR MEMORY

What do you think begins to happen to your
memory right after you have finished learning something?
Does it immediately start forgetting? No! Your brain actually
increases its power and continues remembering. For a short
time after your study session, your brain integrates the
information, making a more complete picture of everything it
has just learned. Only then does the rapid decline in memory
begin, and as much as 80 percent of what you have learned can
be forgotten in a day.

However, if you catch the top of the wave of your memory, and
briefly review (look back over) what you have been studying,
the memory is imprinted far more strongly, and stays at the crest
of the wave for a much longer time. To maximize your brain's
power to remember, take a few minutes at the end of a day and
use a Mind Map to review what you have learned. Then review
it at the end of a week, again at the end of a month, and finally
a week before your test or exam. That way you'll ride your
memory wave all the way there – and beyond!

The Mind Map ®

— A PICTURE OF THE WAY YOU THINK

Do you like taking notes? More important, do you like having
to go back over and learn them before tests or exams? Most
students I know certainly do not! And how do you take your
notes? Most people take notes on lined paper, using blue or
black ink. The result, visually, is boring. And what does *your*
brain do when it is bored? It turns off, tunes out, and goes to
sleep! Add a dash of color, rhythm, imagination, and the whole
note-taking process becomes much more fun, uses more of your
brain's abilities, and improves your recall and understanding.

Generally, your Mind Map is highly personal and need not be
understandable to any other person. It mirrors your brain. Its
purpose is to build up your "memory muscle" by creating
images that will help you recall instantly the most important
points about characters and plot sequences in a work of fiction
you are studying.

You will find Mind Maps throughout this book. Study them, add some color, personalize them, and then try drawing your own. You'll remember them far better. Stick them in your files and on your walls for a quick-and-easy review of the topic.

HOW TO DRAW A MIND MAP

1 First of all, briefly examine the Mind Maps and Mini Mind Maps used in this book. What are the common characteristics? All of them use small pictures or symbols, with words branching out from the illustration.

2 Decide which idea or character in the book you want to illustrate and then draw a picture, starting in the middle of the page so that you have plenty of room to branch out. Remember that no one expects a young Rembrandt or Picasso here; artistic ability is not as important as creating an image that you (and you alone) will remember. A round smiling (or sad) face might work as well in your memory as a finished portrait. Use marking pens of different colors to make your Mind Map as vivid and memorable as possible.

3 As your thoughts flow freely, add descriptive words and other ideas that connect to the central image. Print clearly, using one word per line if possible.

4 Further refine your thinking by adding smaller branching lines, containing less important facts and ideas, to connect with the main points.

5 Presto! You have a personal outline of your thoughts and concepts about the characters and the plot of the story. It's not a stodgy formal outline, but a colorful image that will stick in your mind, it is hoped, throughout classroom discussions and final exams.

HOW TO READ A MIND MAP

1 Begin in the center, the focus of your topic.

2 The words/images attached to the center are like chapter headings; read them next.

3 Always read out from the center, in every direction (even on the left-hand side, where you will have to read from right to left, instead of the usual left to right).

USING MIND MAPS

Mind Maps are a versatile tool; use them
for taking notes in class or from books, for
solving problems, for brainstorming with
friends, and for reviewing and working for tests or exams –
their uses are endless. You will find them invaluable for
planning essays for coursework and exams. Number your main
branches in the order in which you want to use them and off
you go – the main headings for your essay are done and all
your ideas are logically organized.

Preparing for tests and exams

◆ Review your work systematically. Cram at the beginning of
your course, not the end, and avoid "exam panic!"
◆ Use Mind Maps throughout your course, and build a Master
Mind Map for each subject – a giant Mind Map that
summarizes everything you know about the subject.
◆ Use memory techniques such as mnemonics (verses or
systems for remembering things like dates and events).
◆ Get together with one or two friends to study, compare
Mind Maps, and discuss topics.

AND FINALLY...

Have *fun* while you learn – it has been shown that students
who make their studies enjoyable understand and remember
everything better and get the highest grades. I wish you and
your brain every success! (Tony Buzan)

HOW TO USE THIS GUIDE

This guide assumes that you have already read *The Crucible*, although you could read Background and The Story of *The Crucible* before that. It is best to use the guide alongside the play. You could read the Who's Who? and Themes sections without referring to the play, but you will get more out of these sections if you do refer to it to check the points made in these sections, especially when thinking about the questions designed to test your recall and help you to think about the play.

THE DIFFERENT SECTIONS

The Commentary section can be used in a number of ways. One way is to read a section in the play and then read the Commentary for that section. Continue until you come to a test section, test yourself, and then take a break! Or, read the Commentary for a section of the play, then read that section in the play itself, then go back to the Commentary. Find out what works best for you.

Topics for Discussion and Brainstorming gives topics that could well appear on exams or provide the basis for coursework. It would be particularly useful for you to discuss them with friends, or brainstorm them using Mind Map techniques (see p. vii).

How to Get an "A" in English Literature gives valuable advice on what to look for in a text, and what skills you need to develop in order to achieve your personal best.

The Exam Essay is a useful night-before reminder of how to tackle exam questions, and Model Answer and Essay Plan gives an example of an "A"-grade essay and the Mind Map and plan used to write it.

THE QUESTIONS

Whenever you come across a question in the guide with a star ✪ in front of it, think about it for a moment. You could even jot down a few words to focus your mind. There is not usually a "right" answer to these questions; it is important for you to develop your own opinions if you want to get an "A." The Test Yourself sections are designed to take you about 10–20 minutes each. Take a short break after each one.

KEY TO ICONS

Themes

A **theme** is an idea explored by an author. Whenever a theme is dealt with in the guide, the appropriate icon is used. This means you can find where a theme is mentioned just by leafing through the book. Go on – Try it now!

- The individual vs. authority

- The effects of fear

- Integrity

- Mass hysteria

- The corruption of justice

STYLE AND LANGUAGE

This icon is used in the Commentary wherever there is a special section on the author's choice of words and imagery.

 ACKGROUND

Before The Crucible

The playwright Arthur Miller was born in New York on October 17, 1915, to a non-Orthodox Jewish family. Miller had a comfortable childhood, but when his father was ruined in 1929 in the Depression, the family moved to Brooklyn. Arthur Miller's school career was unpromising; he worked briefly in his father's business and then took a variety of casual jobs, some of them manual, which provided the background for several of his plays.

Miller began to read extensively and applied to the University of Michigan to study journalism. As a student he wrote award-winning dramas and began to think of a career in playwriting. After graduating in 1938, he returned to New York, where he worked on various theater projects, but he was eventually forced to return to manual work. In 1940 he married an old college girlfriend. When the United States entered World War II, he was rejected for military service because of an old sports injury.

Miller was beginning to be successful in other forms of writing, but his main interest was in live theater. His first Broadway play won the Theatre Guild National Award but was not a commercial success. During this long apprenticeship, Miller was hammering out the themes central to his best-known work—the link between social commitment and personal integrity, the individual's need to confront his past, and conflict within the family. A chance conversation provided the idea for his first widely acclaimed play, *All My Sons* (1947). *Death of a Salesman* (1949) had an even longer run and was performed worldwide.

The Cold War and Senator McCarthy

After World War II ended, America became locked in political rivalry with Communist Russia (the USSR), the so-called Cold War. The threat of nuclear weapons hung over the two superpowers' struggle for dominance. In June 1950, when Russia's ally, Communist China, began to expand into Southeast Asia, America

1

became involved in the Korean War. This conflict had an enormous effect on the political climate at home. Fear that Communists were infiltrating the government led to the rise of Senator Joseph McCarthy, the most prominent figure in a committee that scrutinized possible suspects. His investigations were aimed particularly at university teachers, trade union members, and artists of all kinds—anyone the committee suspected of left-wing sympathies. Those called before the Un-American Activities Committee were asked to prove their innocence by naming others. Some witnesses caved in; others lost their jobs. There were many suicides, and careers were destroyed when writers who were accused of left-wing sympathies were banned by Hollywood and the television networks.

It was against this background that Miller wrote *The Crucible*. The Salem witch trials had fascinated him long before he saw their possibility as an **allegory** for McCarthyism. The play opened in January 1953, and won two prestigious awards, but the critics were distracted by the obvious parallel with contemporary events.

In 1956 Miller found himself in the same dilemma as his hero, John Proctor. The Committee called on him to testify. When Miller refused to mention names, he was fined and given a suspended prison sentence. The Supreme Court acquitted him a year and a half later. By then the McCarthy hysteria had died down, and Senator McCarthy himself was dead.

In 1956 the divorced Arthur Miller married film star Marilyn Monroe. The marriage lasted barely four years. He married his third wife in 1962. He has continued to enjoy great success with his later writings and is acknowledged as one of the world's greatest living playwrights.

The Crucible

The Crucible is one of Miller's most frequently produced works. As the McCarthy era receded, it became easier to assess the merits of the play and realize that it has a universal significance outside the context of a particular crisis in American history. Miller himself is pleased at this development.

A crucible is a melting pot or vessel in which crude ore is heated to a temperature that makes it release the pure metal. The **metaphor** applies most of all to the hero, John Proctor, who finds his true self by enduring a different kind of purification, but it is almost as apt for several other characters as well as for the whole community that suffered from these tragic events.

Historical background of the play

PURITANS IN NORTH AMERICA

In the late sixteenth and early seventeenth centuries, some English trading companies started to send settlers to North America. Among them were the Pilgrim Fathers, who crossed the Atlantic in the *Mayflower* and landed in Massachusetts on November 21, 1620. Ten years later, about a thousand Puritans settled around Massachusetts Bay, in the area later known as New England. They brought with them a royal charter to set up a colony ruled by a Governor and General Court. A Puritan elite of politicians and clergymen imposed a strict administration on the new colony. As well as reclaiming land from the forest, the settlers had to put up with the Native American tribes and periodic outbreaks of smallpox.

By 1692 there were marked differences between the various centers of population. Trade and education flourished in towns like Boston; inland areas were much less safe and prosperous. Several other factors caused unrest. While the colony awaited the arrival of a new charter from England, its laws, including those on land tenure, were technically suspended. The rulers felt their grasp slipping.

SALEM

The village in the play had developed as the agricultural hinterland of Salem, a thriving trading town on the coast five miles away. Rivers and sea inlets lay between the town and the village, which was in reality a collection of scattered farms. Farmers living further inland had to grow their produce on much less fertile terrain. Added to jealousies about land were disputes over appointing a minister. The town continued to demand taxes and to exercise authority over the villagers.

PURITANISM

Although officially part of the Church of England, the 1630 Puritans were closer in belief and practice to Presbyterian Calvinism. They believed that every soul was predestined for Heaven or Hell. Old Testament law applied to every area of life. The Puritans blamed the Devil for any temptations to break their stern code. Those who broke the rules had to confess in public and suffer severe punishment. To work on Sunday was a serious offense. The Puritans disapproved of most forms of recreation. They confined their reading to the Bible and other religious texts. Children had to live up to this code of behavior from their earliest years and do their share of adult work from the age of seven.

Miller discusses the effects of this highly demanding self-discipline in his notes to Act 1 of *The Crucible*.

WITCHCRAFT

Like most people in the seventeenth century, the Puritans believed in witches. The idea of witchcraft existed long before the Christian era. The Old Testament states, "Thou shalt not suffer a witch to live." This was the basis of the witchcraft laws. In prehistoric societies, magic and sorcery were a feature of religion; the early Christian Church regarded them as the remains of paganism. There were laws against the practice of witchcraft, but no systematic persecution.

Anxieties began to increase when the Church declared in 1320 that magic and witchcraft involved a pact with the Devil and were called heresy, carrying the penalty of eternal damnation. The reformed Protestant Church shared these views. Whereas ordinary people worried about the harm witches might do them, the Church regarded every lost soul as a defeat in the war between God and the Devil. You will notice this difference in *The Crucible*.

During the sixteenth and seventeenth centuries, thousands were put to death for witchcraft. Medicine and veterinary science were so primitive that disease and sudden death could seem to result from a spell cast by a spiteful neighbor. Those suspected of being witches were male and female, of all ages and social ranks, but most of them were elderly women. The most famous handbook on witchcraft was *Malleus Maleficarum* ("The Witches' Hammer"). This might have been one of the books *weighted with authority* that Reverend Hale brings to Salem.

THE SALEM WITCH-HUNT

There were several witchcraft trials in Massachusetts before 1692. Two involved adolescent girls suffering hysterical fits similar to those seen in Salem. In January 1692 the daughter and niece of the village parson, Reverend Parris, having experimented with fortune-telling, began to babble nonsense and twist their limbs into grotesque positions. They claimed that the spirit of Parris's West Indian slave Tituba was tormenting them. Soon, more young girls began to display the same symptoms. Tituba and two other women were arrested on the charge of bewitching them.

Over the following months, the number of hysterical girls increased, as did the number of people they accused. The youngest victim was a child of four. The defendants were jailed, but not tried until June, when the new governor set up his official court, which decided to allow "spectral evidence," that is, the girls' allegation that the witches were sending out their invisible spirits. The witch-hunt spread and scores of people went to prison. Those who confessed were reprieved. Six men and thirteen women were hanged. Since prisoners had to pay for their keep, many families went bankrupt. Doubts arose about the "spectral evidence," particularly when the girls began naming prominent people. The Governor intervened, and in May 1693 the remaining accused were set free, except for those who could not pay their prison charges.

HOW HISTORICALLY ACCURATE IS THE CRUCIBLE?

The Crucible is close to what we know about events in 1692. Much of the dialogue repeats the inquiry documents word for word. Miller made changes for practical dramatic reasons or to emphasize the themes of the play. It will help you to understand *The Crucible* if you think about the reasons for his changes, or, better still, discuss them with your friends. Here are some of them.

All characters in *The Crucible* are taken from official documents, but the number of people involved in the witch-hunt is greatly reduced. The fortune-telling becomes a more dramatic expedition into the Devil-haunted forest. The date when the hysteria began is advanced from winter to spring. Several execution dates are altered; for example, John Proctor did not die with Rebecca Nurse. Miller also standardizes the ages of the girls; with the exception of Betty Parris, they are all teenagers. In reality, they spanned a much wider age range and included several adults.

The only piece of pure invention is the relationship between Abigail Williams and John Proctor. In 1692 he was a man in his sixties and she was a girl of 11. However, the invented relationship rings true to the repression of Puritan society and forms a dynamic center around which the whole story develops.

Such discrepancies are less important than the themes developed in the text. Like all great plays, *The Crucible* speaks to us about universal human issues. The details of place and time are merely the playwright's way of creating his ideas in flesh and blood.

You can take an Internet tour of old Salem village and the witch museum at *www.salemwitchmuseum.com*. There is also a film version of *The Crucible* for which Arthur Miller wrote the screenplay.

Care with context

? Social and historical context is very important with *The Crucible*. Take ten minutes to Mind Map the key points, using the headings given on pp. 3–5 of this guide.

Take a break before brushing up on the plot

THE STORY OF
THE CRUCIBLE

Refer to the story Mind Map on pp. 8–9 while reading this.

One night in 1692, Reverend Samuel Parris, the minister of Salem village, finds his daughter Betty and his niece Abigail **dancing** with their friends in the **forest.** His slave Tituba is also present, casting spells. The play opens a few hours later with Betty lying on her bed and seemingly unable to **wake** up. Rumors of **witchcraft** are already spreading through the village. Mr. Parris is terrified for the effect on his reputation. The entry of various villagers reveals a community split by guilty secrets, personal disputes, and quarrels over land rights. Among them is John Proctor, who has had an affair with **Abigail,** but now wants to break it off. Abigail tells John that the girls were only playing. Rebecca Nurse tries to calm the mounting anxiety, but after the arrival of Reverend **Hale,** a noted **witch-finder,** Mr. and Mrs. Putnam try to exploit the situation for their own ends. To save herself, Abigail blames **Tituba.** Mr. **Hale** forces the terrified **slave** to confess that she made a pact with **the Devil.** She names two other witches. Abigail sees a chance to escape punishment, so she joins in the accusations, supported by the now fully conscious Betty.

Two weeks later, the witch-hunt has intensified. John has tried to keep aloof by working on his farm. His wife, Elizabeth, has heard alarming details from their servant, **Mary Warren,** who was one of the girls in the forest. Now the girls go into **hysterical fits** in court, and anyone whom they accuse is charged with witchcraft. Elizabeth begs John to repeat to the court officials what **Abigail** told him, and to make Abigail realize that their affair is over. She knows that Abigail wants to **accuse** her and **take her place.** John is reluctant to speak out. Elizabeth says he is hesitating because he is still attracted to Abigail. On her return from the village, Mary mentions that Elizabeth's name has come up in court.

Mr. Hale arrives. He is going around to the villagers to test their Christian faith. He is dissatisfied with John's record of

ACT 3

Abigail whips up hysteria in court

John claims the girls are lying

Giles and John are arrested

John destroys his confession and decides to be hanged

ACT 4

Hale begs Elizabeth to make her husband confess

9

church attendance and his inability to repeat all **Ten Commandments.** John's friends, Giles Corey and Francis Nurse (Rebecca's husband), interrupt them. Both their wives have been charged and arrested. Mr. Hale is shocked, but unwilling to intervene. A few minutes later, two court officials arrive, with a warrant to **arrest Elizabeth.** Abigail claims that Elizabeth has sent her spirit out to stab her in the belly. Elizabeth lets herself be taken away, leaving John to threaten Mary that he will make her tell the truth to the judges.

John, Francis, and Giles go to court with Mary to accuse the girls of **fraud.** Judge **Danforth** thinks John is trying to undermine the court and tries to make him withdraw by promising that Elizabeth will not be tried for a year because she is **pregnant.** John refuses to desert his friends. **Giles** says **Mr. Putnam** is using his daughter to accuse his neighbors so that he can **buy up their land.** Giles is arrested when he refuses to name the man who gave him the information. Despite her fear, Mary stands up to Danforth and says that the fits the girls put on in court are **all pretense.** The judge sends for Abigail and her friends. When they try to discredit Mary by pretending to be possessed, John leaps up and confesses **his adultery with Abigail.**

Danforth sends for Elizabeth to ask whether her husband is an adulterer. Unaware that John has already confessed, and to save her husband's reputation, Elizabeth says, "No." Danforth believes that John has lied. Mr. Hale, whose doubts have increased all through the hearing, pleads with Danforth, but the judge is **remorseless.** Abigail stirs up a frenzy that overwhelms everyone in court except John and Mr. Hale. Unable to withstand her pressure, Mary denounces John as the **"Devil's man."** Danforth orders Giles and John to jail.

Three months later, seven people are to be hanged at dawn. Those who confessed have been **reprieved.** Tituba and Sarah Good are moved to another cell so that Mr. Parris can speak to the two judges. He wants Danforth to postpone the executions, hoping that the prisoners will **confess.** The witch-hunt has now spread far beyond Salem, and the province is on the point of revolt. **Abigail** has fled after robbing her **uncle's strongbox.** Mr. Hale enters, bitter and disillusioned; he is counseling the prisoners to **lie** and save their lives. He too asks for a postponement, but Danforth refuses. He sends for Elizabeth, and leaves her alone with John. He feels unworthy to die beside Rebecca and the others and wants to confess. Elizabeth will not advise her husband; she tells him she shares the blame for **his adultery.** John decides to confess, but as he is cross-examined, he realizes that he cannot betray either himself or his fellow prisoners by **signing his name to the paper.** He tears up the confession and goes with Rebecca to the gallows.

now that you know what's what, take a break before seeing who's who

WHO'S WHO?

The Mini Mind Map above summarizes the characters in *The Crucible*. Test yourself by looking at the full Mind Map on p. 23, and then copying the Mini Mind Map and trying to add to it from memory.

To heighten the impression of a whole community in crisis, Miller mentions real-life figures that never appear on stage. For practical reasons he dramatized only twenty-one. The most important are discussed below in order of appearance, followed by a short section on the others.

Reverend Samuel Parris

There is very little good to be said for him. Even allowing the difficulties of such a quarrelsome parish, we have to agree with Miller's judgment. Samuel Parris's guiding principle is self-interest, but he is too ineffective to achieve his purpose. He reacts to events rather than controlling them. His vanity, resentment, and constant complaints against his parishioners betray a weak character. He is servile toward social superiors, but brutal to anyone unable to retaliate, such as Tituba. This may explain why his daughter loses consciousness when he discovers her in the forest.

In the opening scene, Parris shocks us by his lack of fatherly feeling. He is far more concerned about the effects of Betty's illness on himself. His inability to make firm decisions has led him to summon an expert witch-finder, while trying to stop the rumors of witchcraft that would damage his own reputation. When the blame is safely diverted toward Tituba, Mr. Parris becomes an enthusiastic witch-hunter.

His behavior during the trial scenes is as self-centered as we would expect. Parris fears the victims will turn against him if they are set free, and sweats with anxiety whenever the judge seems impressed by their defense. His anxious interruptions provoke a crushing rebuke from Danforth.

Parris gets his comeuppance when his niece realizes that the tide of public opinion has turned against the witch-hunt, and makes a run for it with the contents of his strongbox. When his enemies are condemned to die, he pleads for a postponement—because he fears he may be assassinated, not out of concern for the victims.

Tituba

Tituba is the black slave Parris has brought with him from Barbados. She is affectionate and loyal, despite what seems routine harsh treatment from her master. Abigail blames her for what happened during the girls' expedition into the forest. Tituba's angry protest has no effect; she is made a scapegoat, and, not surprisingly, succumbs to the pressure to confess that she has made a *compact with the Devil*. At the end of the play, we see her in prison with Sarah Good, a homeless old woman also accused of witchcraft.

Tituba's exotic appearance and alien culture are partly responsible for her downfall, but she is not victimized because she is a slave. Like Sarah Good, she is of low social status, with no one to stand up for her. In times of panic, society sometimes singles out those least able to defend themselves.

The historical Tituba was released and sold to pay for the expenses of her imprisonment.

Abigail Williams

Miller gives us two facts about Abigail: She is *strikingly beautiful* and she has an *endless capacity for dissembling*. Abigail is one of a group of Salem girls, most of whom are orphans. Their childhood has been joyless, subject to strict Puritan discipline. Although adolescent, these girls are addressed as "child," a deliberate suppression of their developing sexuality. They suffer the drudgery of adult labor without adult freedom. They cannot work off their energies in the outdoor pursuits available to their brothers, nor express their frustrations. Their rebellion takes the form of expeditions into the danger zone of the forest. The thrill of arousing adult anxiety if they are discovered is probably part of the excitement.

Before *The Crucible* begins, John Proctor has drawn Abigail into the adult world by seducing her. *"I look for John Proctor that took me from my sleep and put knowledge in my heart!"* she cries, when John rejects her. His repentance is sincere enough, even if it does not stretch to what he has done to his 17-year-old servant. Elizabeth sees her adulterous husband as *a good man ... only somewhat bewildered*, while Abigail is a *whore*. ✪ How far has society changed in its judgment of men and women?

As well as being the driving force of the play, Abigail's desire for John is a symbol for the anarchic, irrational side of life that the Puritans tried so hard to repress. Thwarted love makes her ruthless. She has already drunk *a charm to kill John Proctor's wife*. By blaming Tituba for the adventure in the forest, Abigail discovers a more dangerous aspect to the ascendancy she holds over her friends. When she begins to name the witches, Betty picks up her lead without any instruction. Backed up by her hysterical followers, Abigail controls the adults who have previously controlled her. Her ability to turn events to her own advantage increases with practice.

Her refusal to accept John's rejection combines fatally with the rising social panic. The accusations eventually bring down her real target, Elizabeth Proctor. Once embarked on this course, Abigail cannot pull back, even when the man she wants is condemned to die. In the end, all she can do is to leave town in a hurry. With a last bold gesture she ensures a comfortable future by emptying her uncle's strongbox.

Abigail has courage, intelligence, and a magnetic personality, but employs these gifts only in destructive ways. She exerts a totally evil influence on the terrified villagers. Most of them do not realize that the only "witch" in their midst is Abigail Williams.

John Proctor

John Proctor is the main character of the play, the **protagonist.** He appears first as one of the villagers drawn to Parris's house by the rumor of Betty's strange illness. His entrance comes directly after Betty's cry to Abigail, *"You drank a charm to kill John Proctor's wife!"*

Almost until the end of the play, a sense of guilt and shame holds John back from taking positive action at the right moment. In his scene with Abigail, we learn the reasons for his guilt and why he lies to himself as well as to Abigail and his wife. *"I have hardly stepped off my farm this seven-month."*

In the scene around Betty's bed, John emerges as a down-to-earth man who speaks his mind and is not afraid to confront those in authority, especially when they abuse their position. We may disapprove of his threatening Abigail and Mary with the whip, but this must be seen in the context of his time. His heated replies to Mr. Parris are not always to be taken at face value (*"Why, then I must find it and join it."*) They show an honest disgust at Parris's materialistic outlook and betrayal of his calling.

John is a practical farmer, struggling to earn a living for his family, but he still finds time to take a sensuous delight in his surroundings: *"I never see such a load of flowers on the earth."* The problems with his marriage appear insurmountable, but finally they appear as superficial damage to what has been a deep and lasting union.

John's anguished reaction to his wife's arrest is the first move toward breaking through the restraints imposed by guilt. In the escalating horror of the witch-hunt, he becomes a reluctant hero. In striving to expose its fraud, he comes to acknowledge his responsibility to society and finds his true self.

Miller has sometimes been criticized for giving his hero a modern mind. This is surely a misreading of history. By 1692 there was dissent at all levels of colonial society. The number of recorded whippings, reprimands, and public humiliations prove that many people did not accept the Puritan ethic. John Proctor in Miller's play is a link between our own times and the values of seventeenth-century Massachusetts.

Mr. and Mrs. Putnam

The Putnams are an unattractive couple. Mrs. Putnam takes a gloating pleasure in the rumors of witchcraft. This cannot be completely accounted for by her obsession with finding a scapegoat for her inability to bear healthy children. Our sympathy for her loss shrinks when we learn that she has sent her daughter to consult spirits and when we see her turn on gentle Rebecca Nurse, who has come to offer advice. Thomas Putnam gives Rebecca a touchy reply: *"I am one of nine sons; the Putnam seed have peopled this province."* It suggests there may be secret reproaches at home, and that the couple has united to throw the blame elsewhere.

Thomas Putnam is important in village society, with narrowly conformist opinions. He supports Mr. Parris because he is an authority figure, but despises him as a man. Both Putnams make use of Parris to stir up the witch-hunt. Mr. Putnam has a falling out with John Proctor early in the play over his poor attendance at church. He also quarrels with John and Giles Corey over land rights. He is responsible for many of the accusations of witchcraft, and exploits them to acquire even more land. The fact that both Mr. and Mrs. Putnam use their daughter to further their own ends tells us a great deal about them as parents.

Mary Warren

The same age as Abigail (17), Mary is the most fully developed character among the group of girls. She is *subservient, naive, lonely*, and when we first meet her she is in a panic about their escapade in the forest. She is a target for bullying, yet, for such a timid person, she is surprisingly flippant to her master, perhaps because she knows his secret. (This comes out at the end of Act 2.)

Mary's behavior varies greatly during the play. At the beginning of Act 2, Elizabeth tells John that she has been unable to stop Mary from leaving the house: *"She raises up her chin like the daughter of a prince and says to me, 'I must go to Salem ... I am an official of the court!' "* The attention of Judge Danforth and other officials has inflated Mary's ego, but her sense of self-importance is fragile. When she enters, she is depressed and exhausted. She weeps for the sentence passed on Goody Osburn. Her conscience protests, but she is too fearful to question the judges' version of events. This inner conflict has made her seek comfort in a childish pursuit— dollmaking. The "poppet" (rag doll) she sews in court has fatal consequences for the Proctors.

When her master orders her to bed, Mary becomes petulant and tries to assert her rights; but by the end of the act, she is sobbing in terror at the thought of standing up to Abigail: *"I cannot, I cannot."* Despite her best efforts, this is exactly what happens in Act 3.

Mary represents all those people who recognize injustice but are too weak to resist it. Through her, Miller also shows how and why the girls managed to believe in their victims' guilt. Look particularly at her speeches to John and Elizabeth in Act 2 and Act 3 (*"I – cannot faint now"*).

Rebecca Nurse

More than anyone else in the play, Rebecca shows up the shocking irrationality of the witch-hunt. She is an elderly woman, highly respected in the community for her charitable works and genuine goodness. She represents the best of the Puritan way of life without its negative and destructive side. Betty feels Rebecca's calming influence as soon as she sits at her bed. Rebecca tries to steer Proctor away from his confrontation with Parris and warns her neighbors, *"There is prodigious danger in the seeking of loose spirits."* The Putnams override her common sense, and Rebecca falls victim to the malicious jealousy of Ann Putnam. In the last act, Rebecca's quiet faith and courage help Proctor make his final decision to go to the scaffold. Miller's portrait accurately reflects the historical reality of the woman whose monument forms the chief feature of the Salem 1992 Memorial.

Giles Corey

A crank and a nuisance, but withal a deeply innocent and brave man, Giles is a tough, argumentative old farmer of 83. He speaks without thinking and has a total disregard for other people's opinions. His unacknowledged deafness has intensified these traits. Giles's friends forgive his irritating side for the sake of his courage and honesty. His thoughtlessness makes him his own worst enemy. A casual inquiry about his wife's scholarly habits ends in her being taken to the gallows.

Giles's encounter with Judge Danforth in Act 3 illustrates almost all aspects of his quirky nature. He is naively pleased with Danforth's compliments, and does not realize until too late that the judge has outmaneuvered him. Giles has accused Thomas Putnam of using the witch-hunt to acquire other people's land. Very rashly, he offers an unsupported allegation as evidence. When asked to identify his informant, Giles loses his temper, haggles over a legal point, and refuses to give the man's name. He is arrested for contempt of court.

The way Giles dies perfectly sums up his life. He refuses to plead in court, and rather than change his mind, he allows himself to be crushed to death under a pile of stones. With no plea, and therefore no trial or verdict, the court cannot forfeit his land, and it will pass to his sons.

Reverend John Hale

The minister from Beverly is perhaps the most pitiable character in the play. Although John Proctor's road to self-knowledge ends at the gallows, he dies with a renewed sense of his own worth and reconciled with his wife. In Reverend Hale's case, self-knowledge brings a weight of guilt that must haunt him for the rest of his life.

John Hale is a sincere and kindly man. His failing is to believe without question that those who rule by the laws of God cannot make mistakes and that all evil is external, not in people's minds. He confuses authority with those who administer it. By the end of the play, he has realized that the powerful can be imperfect. A rather conceited intellectual, and inclined to *smile at the ignorance of the yeomanry*, he is so eager to use *his painfully acquired armory of symptoms, catchwords, and diagnostic procedures*, that without meaning to, he unleashes the Salem witch-hunt.

Hale questions Tituba with conscientious attention to detail; he even treats her kindly. It is plain that her fear prompts her to "confess" and that Parris and Putnam are taking callous advantage of her, but Hale is too blind to notice. By Act 2, the witch-hunt he has authorized is out of control. When he interviews the Proctors, he firmly suppresses his emerging doubts. He convinces himself that the arrest of Rebecca Nurse indicates *some secret blasphemy that stinks to Heaven* and not a miscarriage of justice.

Reverend Hale's doubts grow as the trials proceed. In Act 3, he becomes increasingly alarmed and tries to make a case for the defense. Danforth ignores his attempts. When Elizabeth is removed, Hale breaks into open opposition: *"I may shut my conscience to it no more—private vengeance is working through this testimony."* After John Proctor's arrest he denounces the proceedings and walks out.

Tortured by remorse, Mr. Hale returns to Salem and tries to persuade the condemned prisoners to avoid hanging by making a false confession. *"Cleave to no faith when faith brings blood,"* he warns Elizabeth, begging her to make her husband confess. She rejects Hale's plea as *the Devil's argument*. The minister's last desperate appeal proves that he has lost sight of everything but his own sense of guilt.

Elizabeth Proctor

Early in the play Abigail describes Elizabeth as *a bitter woman, a lying, cold, snivelling woman ... a gossiping liar*. We soon learn the true reasons for her opinion, and when Elizabeth appears in Act 2, it becomes obvious that Abigail has grossly distorted the truth.

Elizabeth has a more complex personality than her quiet, somewhat repressed manner suggests. John's infidelity has hurt both her pride and her religious convictions. She cannot bring herself to give her husband the warmth he craves, and she suspects, quite rightly, that he still finds Abigail attractive. She undervalues John's efforts to make amends.

Elizabeth is both gentle and practical. Despite her pity for the *poor rabbit*, she kills and cooks it for John's supper. She tries to save Mary a whipping; after her arrest, she gives orders for the household and tries to conceal her fear, concerned more for the children than herself. She is the first to understand Abigail's intentions and braves her husband's anger to urge him into action. Unfortunately, it is already too late.

During her three months in prison, Elizabeth looks into her heart and realizes that her own coldness has provoked John's adultery. *"I never knew how I should say my love. I kept a cold house!"* ❂ When did Elizabeth realize this truth? It must surely be before she tells the court that her husband is not an adulterer. Going against all her beliefs, she lies to save her husband's reputation, unaware that he has already made his adultery public.

Elizabeth's real strength shines through in the last act. She resists all pressure from John himself, from court officials, and her own longing to save him from the gallows. She insists that her husband must decide for himself and makes no comment on his first false choice. She gives way to grief only when he has torn up his confession.

Judge Danforth

Danforth, the senior judge, is *a grave man in his sixties, of some humor and sophistication.* His reasonable manner only reinforces the horror of his actions in Salem. Only once does he lose control of himself, when at the end of the trial scene he becomes caught up in the hysteria created by Abigail.

At the beginning of Act 4, Danforth hears from a distraught Mr. Parris that Abigail has fled from Salem with the contents of his strongbox. *He walks in thought, deeply worried.* Is Danforth worried that Abigail is a fraud, and the whole series of trials has been based on a false assumption? No, he is anxious that the news may get around and persuade others to think so.

To the very end of the play, Danforth remains convinced that he is in the right. *"While I speak God's law, I will not crack its voice with whimpering."* Like Mr. Hale before his change of heart, he seems to believe that the witchcraft hysteria and its results are in themselves a sign that the Devil is at work in Salem.

Through Deputy-Governor Danforth, Miller demonstrates what happens when the state assumes absolute moral authority to direct the lives and beliefs of its citizens. The results are terrifying. Danforth "knows" that his mission is to purge the village. This overrides legal quibbles about evidence or court proceedings. He is unable to understand that even if God's law is infallible, its interpreters are not.

This throws light on his behavior in Act 3, where he displays both ruthlessness and courtesy. Judge Danforth and the defendants are following different agenda. John and Giles suppose that their fate depends on presenting credible evidence. Danforth has a higher good in mind. He must carry out God's will in Salem. To this end he manipulates court procedure and openly exploits the weaknesses of those on trial. He uses Elizabeth's pregnancy in his efforts to dissuade John from charging the girls with fraud, and he remains silent while Hathorne bullies Mary Warren. For the same reason, he will not postpone the hangings. Danforth will not permit any crack in God's fortress.

The overall result is that lies are taken as truth, and common sense ignored, for example his willful blindness to the widespread fear his court has aroused in the village, and his refusal to believe that Elizabeth has lied to spare her husband's reputation. In these incidents Miller drives home the danger of allowing the state to take over the functions of private

The other characters

conscience.

Judge Hathorne, *a bitter, remorseless Salem judge,* typifies the more obvious prejudice of the court. He never attempts to listen to the evidence. Even before he appears, we overhear him trying to entrap Martha Corey. He calls for Giles and Francis to be arrested for contempt, and is the first to insist that Giles should name his informant. He bullies Mary Warren unmercifully and becomes openly hostile to Mr. Hale once the minister has denounced the court. His hectoring manner and lack of judicial seriousness make him a good foil to Deputy-Governor Danforth.

Francis Nurse is Rebecca's husband.

Betty Parris (Parris's daughter, mysteriously unable to wake up), **Mercy Lewis** (*fat, sly, merciless*), and **Susanna Walcott** (*nervous, hurried*) represent what was, in fact, a much larger group of *crazy children* in Salem. Betty is a pathetic, frightened 10-year-old, the first to follow Abigail's lead in naming the "witches." Susanna and Mercy are about the same age as Abigail. Susanna is the doctor's servant. Mercy works for the Putnams. She was seen by Parris dancing naked in the woods, and flees with Abigail at the end of the play.

Hopkins is the Salem jailer. **Cheever** and **Herrick** are minor officials of the court, but, typically, they plead that they are acting under orders. Through them Miller shows that authoritarian systems flourish through the cooperation of ordinary people.

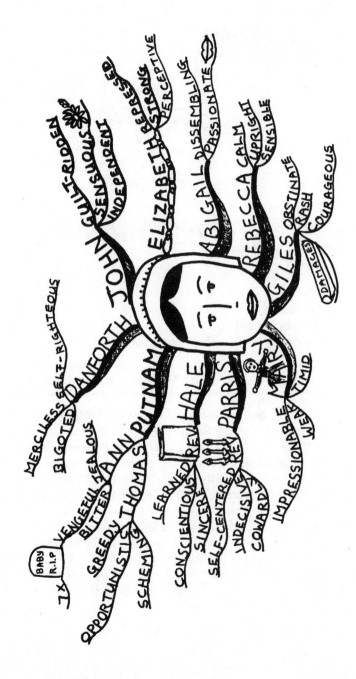

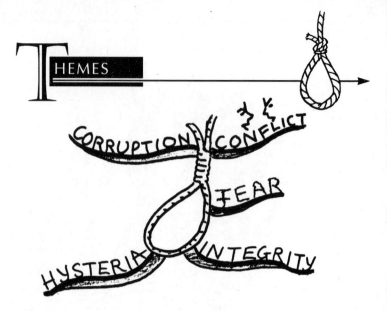

THEMES

A **theme** is an idea developed or explored throughout a work. The main themes of *The Crucible* are shown in the Mini Mind Map above. Test yourself by copying it, adding to it, and then comparing your results with the version on p. 33.

The individual vs. authority

Miller's concept of the parallel between 1950s America and seventeenth-century Salem emerges most clearly in the **themes** of his play. In both cases, Government assumed the right to control citizens' beliefs as well as their actions; in both, the consequences were the same. The reality of Communism and the generally accepted nonreality of witchcraft are beside the point. In *The Crucible*, John and Rebecca are not standing up for individual rights in the modern sense. Salem villagers all believe in witches and the infallibility of the Bible. What the victims oppose is the abuse of power. This is relevant to any age or culture. In late seventeenth-century New England, *the balance began to turn to greater individual freedom*. This did not please the rulers.

Until the eighteenth century, religion played a large part in the running of most European states or colonies. In particular, those affected by the Protestant Reformation conformed to some form of theocratic ("god-ruled") system. Laws were based on the authority of the Bible, and the Church used them to control every aspect of people's lives. The modern idea that religious belief is a matter of private conscience would have been considered blasphemous. Nevertheless, even in seventeenth-century New England, a more tolerant and diversified society was emerging. This movement toward change stirred up great social tensions.

The Reformation had made people more responsible for their own salvation. It substituted public disapproval for the penances of the Catholic Church, yet the wealthier frequently escaped punishment. ❂ Why? In *The Crucible*, Mrs. Putnam is never disciplined for using witchcraft to find out who "killed" her babies.

In Act 1 ("*I have trouble enough ... He says there's a party*"), John Proctor shows his resentment when Parris criticizes his infrequent church attendance. He is absent for practical reasons—Elizabeth's illness, his own work, and no doubt the ten-mile walk. He feels Parris does not deserve respect. Rebecca, more obedient, knows that Parris is unworthy, but is still shocked by John's remarks. Reverend Hale later reprimands him for daring to question Parris's God-given authority.

Act 2 demonstrates the helplessness of people who try to stand up for their rights in a theocratic state. Once the witch-hunt has started, the potential for conflict escalates. Anyone who doubts the so-called evidence is questioning God's will. The judges' handling of the trial relates more to corruption of justice. They cling so inflexibly to their point of view that such law-abiding characters as Rebecca and Francis Nurse are pushed into defiance. Even Hale, an establishment figure, finds he is unable to ignore his conscience. He finally denounces the court. Those whose honesty is stronger than their fear of death inevitably destroy themselves. Rebecca refuses to damn her soul with a lie; Giles values his land more than his life and willingly accepts a horrible death.

The effects of fear

Fear is a dominant emotion in *The Crucible*. Mr. Parris is afraid that his rebellious parishioners will use Betty's strange illness to oust him from his position; Abigail fears that Reverend Hale will find out what she did in the forest, so she embarks on an elaborate hoax that almost destroys the village. Ashamed to confess his affair with Abigail, John Proctor speaks up too late. This is only to say that the villagers of Salem are like people everywhere – they have secrets to hide and worry about their reputations.

The unique feature that drew Miller to Salem was the fear that erupted there in 1692. Puritans believed that the Devil was constantly working to tempt human beings away from God. At the end of the play, Tituba is waiting for Satan to transport her to the *singin' and dancin' in Barbados*. All other references to witchcraft are connected with fear, suspicion, and the collapse of normal social values. The stricken community can no longer defend itself or protect vulnerable individuals.

There are two types of accusation in the play. The first comes from characters seeking revenge or exploiting the panic for personal gain. Others pass on the blame for their misfortunes, but they are not necessarily malicious. Irrational fear deludes them into believing whatever they are told. (No one ever stops to ask why Rebecca should want to harm Mrs. Putnam's babies.) ✪ Think of examples of these types of behavior.

In both the McCarthy trials and the Salem witch-hunt, victims could escape punishment if they denounced others. Supplying names would of course imply that the accused were guilty themselves. In both episodes, only the strongest stood up to their judges. In his autobiography, *Timebends*, Miller describes his reaction to friends who were called up before the McCarthy tribunal and saved themselves by denouncing others. Similarly, in *The Crucible*, we meet characters who confess to practicing witchcraft and accuse others of doing the same. This is the second type of accusation.

Tituba is the first to be interrogated. Mr. Putnam's threat of hanging produces the desired answer, and thereafter the demoralized slave repeats any names suggested to her. Miller builds a prolonged scene around this minor character to show exactly how the prosecutors went about their business. Tituba represents all who were terrified into naming the "witches." (See p. 47, for details.)

The pressures of irrational fear are most vividly illustrated in their effects on Mary Warren. Mary is terrified from the moment she steps inside the court, but she bears up well under cross-examination. Encouraged by Proctor, she refuses to withdraw her claim that the girls are fraudulent, even when bullied by Judge Hathorne, yet she begins to crumple as soon as Abigail sets the girls loose on her. Within minutes, Mary is caught up in their hysteria and she disintegrates. In her final moments on stage, she rushes for protection to the very person responsible for her ordeal.

Integrity

John Proctor's progress to self-awareness represents a major theme running throughout Miller's work. Miller wrote: *I understand the symbolic meaning of a character and his career to consist of the kind of commitment he makes to life or refuses to make* (Introduction to *Collected Plays*). In Miller's thinking, moral honesty cannot be separated from a commitment to society.

In Act 4, the hero cries out, *"God in Heaven, what is John Proctor?"* He finds his answer during his final moments on earth. As in several other Miller plays, the central figure must come to terms with the consequences of past actions. In *The Crucible*'s opening scenes, Proctor takes little interest in the outbreak of hysteria in Salem. He is a busy farmer living five miles from the meetinghouse, and his irritation with Parris has kept him away from church services. Perhaps we should also give him credit for trying to keep away from Abigail, even if his efforts are not successful.

We see him next in his domestic surroundings, ashamed of his adultery, but also resentful that his wife will not accept his sincere repentance. His refusal to meddle in village affairs follows from a very natural reluctance to publicize his adultery. (It later turns out that at least one of Abigail's friends knows about it.) At this stage, John's practical reasons for standing aloof also give him a pretext for evading social responsibility.

When the witch-hunters invade his home and arrest his wife, he is forced to become involved. In the court scenes, John rises above his own fears and resentment to argue as well as he can for common sense and reason. We see his growing social involvement when he turns down the chance to save Elizabeth by abandoning his friends and their wives, yet his plan of action still depends on making someone else take responsibility—Mary Warren. Only when this hope collapses does he tell the full truth, regardless of the consequences.

Act 4 concentrates almost completely on this current theme. John faces a final temptation to retreat into dishonesty and save his life. His newfound closeness with Elizabeth increases his agony. At first he uses his own guilt to escape the gallows, but under Danforth's relentless pressure he arrives at a clear view of what his choice must be. He manages to accept and forgive his own imperfections. Discovering his "core" and identity, John can at last take charge of his life, neither rejecting social involvement nor handing over his conscience to someone else.

Irony is often used in *The Crucible* to emphasize the irrationality of the witch-hunt. That John Proctor's life-affirming choice should lead to death is the greatest irony of the play.

Two other characters, Reverend Hale and Elizabeth, take a similar path to self-awareness. Elizabeth perceives that her own physical coldness was partly responsible for the affair between Abigail and her husband. However, this is a dramatic device to allow John Proctor to come to terms with himself. We have no clue as to how Elizabeth will deal with her knowledge after John's death.

In the final act, Hale is full of remorse for supporting the witch-hunt. Preaching a doctrine that is the exact opposite of his former beliefs, he urges the prisoners to lie in order to save themselves. This desperate attempt to appease his conscience brings him no comfort. He is a man broken by guilt; there is no indication that he will ever recover.

Mass hysteria

Mass hysteria does not have to involve hysterical behavior in the ordinary sense. The phrase describes what happens when the same strong emotion grips a large group of people. Most of us have experienced it in milder forms. When we cheer on our favorite team, feeling part of the crowd intensifies our emotion. This can apply to any situation, even when people are not physically assembled in the same place.

There is another side to the phenomenon. When fear and prejudice spread through a community, they become self-reinforcing and their effect on individuals is enormously magnified. In *The Crucible*, the behavior of both adolescents and adults is a powerful demonstration of this reality. Everything happens against a background of ongoing quarrels that have never been settled. In Act 1, several random circumstances combine to provoke the disaster. The girls' reaction when their expedition to the forest is discovered leads to the suspicion of witchcraft; Mr. Hale is eager to try out his skills; Mrs. Putnam has never stopped grieving for her dead babies, and uses the crisis to find a scapegoat.

By the end of Act 1, the adults have succumbed to their fear that the Devil and his witches are trying to destroy Salem. The only two strong enough to resist—Rebecca and John Proctor—have left the stage. This is the first of the play's biting ironies: The true model of Satanic possession is not the innocent victims, but the accusers (and later, the judges), who hand themselves over to *the little crazy children*.

Once the hysteria is established, it triggers almost every incident in the play. Through the Proctors' servant, Mary Warren, it invades the quiet domesticity of their home. Tragically, the quarrel between John and Elizabeth has a direct effect on their ability to resist. Their dispute prevents John from taking steps that might have changed the course of events.

We know that common sense has lost when we hear about the arrest of so widely respected a person as Rebecca Nurse.

The girls' unpredictable behavior is both a symbol of the hysteria infecting society and a dramatization of that hysteria in action, as well as the gullibility of adults who swallow the girls' accusations. Notice how skillfully Miller leads up to his two scenes of "possession," the first engineered by Abigail to save her own skin, and the second a full-blown demonstration of mass hysteria in action.

At the end of Act 1, we see Abigail whipping Betty Parris into a state of hysteria as she begins a campaign to save herself and, later, to destroy Elizabeth Proctor. In Act 2 we hear about the girls' increasing power, but only through description. Wherever Abigail walks, *the crowd will part like the sea for Israel*, and if her followers *scream and howl and fall to the floor—the person's clapped in the jail for bewitchin' them.* At some point—Miller does not say when—the girls' fraud takes over and they can no longer help their behavior. The playwright skillfully holds back the second scene of possession until the moment of maximum impact—the terrifying climax to Act 3.

There have been several attempts to explain the behavior of the girls at Salem. One theory relates it to Sigmund Freud's work on clinical hysteria. Freud concluded that buried emotions were responsible for symptoms in his patients that appeared to have no physical cause. What he described came very close to what happened at Salem. The symptoms were catching, and Freud's patients were often in a state of "dual consciousness." They knew what was happening to them, but had virtually no control over themselves.

For a precise link with *The Crucible,* look at Mary's speeches— *"I feel a misty coldness climbin' up my back ..."* and *"It were only sport in the beginning, sir ..."*—where she struggles to explain her own state of "dual consciousness."

Miller leaves open the question of how many girls were similarly affected and when this happened. Abigail alone knows exactly what she is doing; she controls the court officials as tightly as she controls her followers. She is confident enough to threaten Judge Danforth, the Deputy-Governor. Danforth thunders at Mary, *"You will confess yourself or you will hang,"* but Abigail instinctively moves on to something far more sinister. Mary ceases to exist in human form when Abigail "sees" her as the yellow bird perched on a roof beam. Psychological torture works by alienating victims from their own identity. In the horrifying climax, Abigail hypnotizes the girls into a single mass consciousness, and uses them to destroy Mary's personality and willpower.

The corruption of justice

It is hard for anyone today to regard a trial for witchcraft as anything other than a mockery of justice. To pick out what goes wrong in *The Crucible* we have to put aside disbelief and look at the details of charging, arrest, and trial.

Reverend Hale discovers the first "witch"—Tituba—without any judicial inquiry at all. The first barrier against an unbiased examination of evidence is the close association of Church and State. Those who interpret God's laws do not imagine themselves capable of human error. As a clergyman in a theocratic society, Mr. Hale is allowed to speak on behalf of the state, although he has no legal training. It is through him that Abigail and her followers become linked to the court as official witch-finders. *"The entire contention of the state ... is that the voice of Heaven is speaking through the children,"* Danforth tells Proctor. Yet the haphazard nature of the accusations leaves them wide open to abuse by people like Thomas Putnam.

The process of arrest is chaotic as well as brutal, as we see when Cheever and Herrick arrive at the Proctors' farmhouse to take Elizabeth to jail. Cheever will not tell her why he is looking for "poppets." During the trials, Danforth manipulates both defendants and legal procedure to suit his purpose. He never attempts to look at probabilities or weigh the defendants' motives. Despite his authority and experience, he presides over an unruly court. He allows Hathorne to score points based on sheer verbal trickery—*"How do you know, then, that you are not a witch?"* Danforth does the same himself when he

31

entraps Elizabeth into lying to save her husband's reputation. He also uses leading questions to get the answers that suit him (though not always successfully):

> *"Might it be that here we have no afflicting spirit loose, but in the court there were some?"*
> *"You deny every scrap and tittle of this?"*
> *"You have seen the Devil, have you not?"*

The greatest injustice in the whole conduct of the witch trials is that the inquisitors offer a reprieve to those who confess, provided they name other suspects. Proctor points out the obvious consequences to Hale, but the minister refuses to face the truth. So the witch-hunt swells to an enormous size and infects other parts of the province. The nightmare ends only when the whole community is on the brink of revolt.

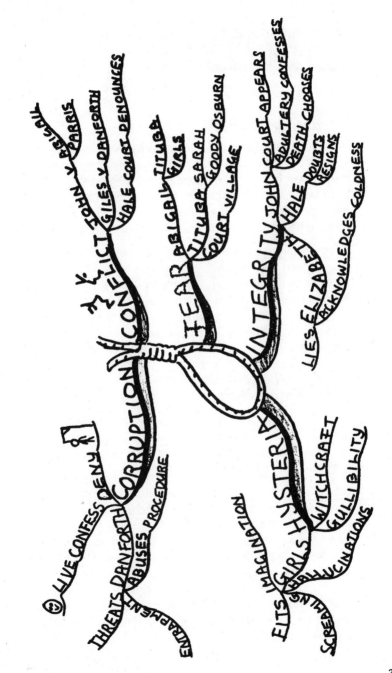

33

STRUCTURE, STYLE, AND LANGUAGE

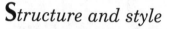

Structure and style

Compared with some of Miller's other plays, *The Crucible* is a straightforward work written in a traditional way. Events on stage occur in order and occupy roughly the same amount of time as they would in real life. In this type of realistic drama, the playwright will concentrate on important episodes and fill in what happens between acts as unobtrusively as possible.

The internal structure of *The Crucible* is, of course, far more complicated than this. Miller employs a different pattern of pace and climax in each act and unifies all four by interweaving John Proctor's personal history with the fate of Salem village. Act 1 is "an overture." The main characters introduce themselves as neighbors invading Mr. Parris's house to ask about the rumors of witchcraft. Their rapid entrances and exits create an atmosphere of anxiety and turmoil. In the midst of this, the scene between John and Abigail alerts us to another story line, but the topic of witchcraft remains dominant.

Act 2, in contrast, opens quietly and explores at length a different situation: the relationship between John and his wife. These two perspectives are brought together when the court officials burst in to arrest Elizabeth.

Structurally, Act 3 is the most complicated section of the entire play. Miller does not place his trial scene in the courtroom itself. We briefly overhear what is happening there, and then, by a natural sequence of events, judges and defendants remove themselves to an anteroom on stage. Thus, Miller can bring into play the cut and thrust of legal drama, but in a much freer setting. In this act, there is also a striking example of what he calls *the holding back of climax.* The Commentary examines in detail how Miller delays and prolongs the presentation of Mary Warren's evidence.

After the uproar of the court comes the chilly isolation of the Salem jail. In Act 4, the witchcraft theme gives way entirely to the resolution of John Proctor's personal crisis. It is a proof of Miller's dramatic skill in blending the public and personal themes of his play that the transition seems entirely natural.

Language

One of the most remarkable aspects of *The Crucible* is Miller's creation of believable dialogue for his seventeenth-century Puritans. Although partly based on what he found in the Salem records, most of it is his own invention. It is convincingly old-fashioned, without being hard to understand. It is a language that carries echoes of the King James Bible, but word by word, apart from a few archaic terms—such as "harlot" and "poppet"—the vocabulary is essentially modern. Miller achieves his effects by linking words in an unusual way, using double negatives, changing verb tenses, and other devices of the same kind. Here are some examples:

> *"He cannot discover no medicine for it in his books;"*
> *"I know you have not opened with me;"*
> *"Seeing I do live so closely with you, they dismissed it;"*
> *"I am thirty-three time in court in my life;"*
> *"He give me nine pound damages;"*
> *"You wonder yet if rebellion's spoke?"*

Within this shared language, Miller varies the way his characters speak to suit their background and personality. Ministers and judges naturally use more elaborate phrases than the villagers. Giles Corey is blunt and even coarse: *"A fart on Thomas Putnam, that is what I say to that!"* John Proctor utters some of the most poetic lines in the play, whether describing his delight in the Massachusetts countryside, or crying out in despair at the end of Act 3.

Most characters use **simile** and **metaphor.** *"There be no blush about my name,"* Abigail reassures her uncle. Judge Danforth tells the children, *"A very augur bit* [a corkscrew-like tool] *will now be turned into your souls until your honesty is proved."* *"My daughter and my niece I discovered dancing like heathen in the forest." "I know how you ... sweated like a stallion whenever I come near!"*

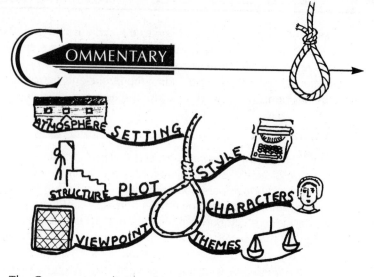

The Commentary divides the play into short sections, beginning with a brief preview that will prepare you for the section and help in last-minute review. The Commentary discusses whatever is important in the section, focusing on the areas shown in the Mini Mind Map above.

ICONS

Wherever there is a focus on a particular theme, the icon for that theme appears in the margin (see p. xi for key). Look out, too, for the Style and Language icons. Being able to comment on style and language will help you to get an "A" on your exam.

You will learn more from the Commentary if you use it alongside the play itself. Read a section from the play, then the corresponding Commentary section—or the other way around.

QUESTIONS

Remember that whenever a question appears in the Commentary with a star ✪ in front of it, you should stop and think about it for a moment. And **remember to take a break** after completing each exercise.

Act 1 Spring 1692, a bedroom in Reverend Samuel Parris's house

Interspersed in the text of Act 1 you will find some extra notes on the characters and some of the general issues raised by the play. Read them carefully. When you are familiar with the text, try to relate individual sections to scenes from the play. For instance, you might link the comments on Thomas Putnam with Giles's accusation against him.

Section 1

◆ The child who cannot wake.
◆ The girls dancing in the forest.
◆ Why did Abigail leave the Proctors?

A MYSTERIOUS ILLNESS

In a small upper bedroom, the Salem minister, Reverend Parris, is praying frantically over the motionless body of his daughter. She is alive, but cannot wake up. Sunlight streaming through the window gives the darker interior an air of confinement. The minister's slave Tituba enters and inquires anxiously about her beloved Betty—and is furiously dismissed by her master. Next to appear is Parris's niece, 17-year-old Abigail. She tells him that Susanna Walcott has brought a message from Dr. Griggs. *"He cannot discover no medicine for it in his books."* This reliance on the authority of "books" will become a leading issue in the play.

The doctor thinks that *unnatural things* might be involved. It is ominous that the first allusion to witchcraft comes from someone we would expect to look for natural causes. Reverend Parris strenuously rebuts Dr. Griggs's suggestion; both uncle and niece tell Susanna to go home without discussing Betty's illness in the village: *"Speak nothing of unnatural causes."* Nevertheless, Parris has sent for another minister, an expert on demonology. ✪ What does this tell us about him? Abigail reminds her uncle that their parlor is full of people talking about witchcraft. She advises him to go down and crush the rumor himself.

"WHAT DID YOU DO WITH HER IN THE FOREST?"

Abigail is not so sensible as she first seemed. We learn that Reverend Parris has caught her with his daughter and other girls dancing around a fire in the forest. *The Salem folk believed that the virgin forest was the Devil's last preserve* and dancing was in itself shocking to the Puritans. We assume this happened during the previous night, since Betty has not been able to move *since midnight*. Abigail protests that her uncle's sudden appearance made Betty faint with terror. She denies that they *trafficked with spirits*, yet one of the girls was naked, he insists. Abigail denies this too—another lie, as we soon find out.

Abigail's ability to stand up for herself and tell convincing lies accounts for her future power over the villagers and Boston judges. Parris accepts her answers very easily. He is afraid his enemies may use the incident to get rid of him. *"My ministry's at stake, my ministry and perhaps your cousin's life."* ✪ What is significant about the word order here?

He asks, *"Your name in the town—it is entirely white, is it not?"* This is the first mention of "name" in the sense of "reputation." ✪ How is Abigail's reputation connected with her uncle's present worries? He inquires why the Proctors sent her away, and why no other family has hired her during the past seven months. Abigail indignantly denounces Goody (Elizabeth) Proctor as a gossiping liar who tried to make her work like a slave. *"Do you begrudge me my bed, uncle?"* she demands. She will use this trick of defending herself with a challenge to great effect in Act 3.

Some questions before meeting the Putnams

?   Why did the Salemites turn up at their minister's house? Was it out of curiosity, to sympathize, to seek reassurance, or something else?

?   What do you deduce from the facts that in this small community no one else would employ Abigail, but Parris doesn't know why?

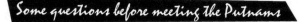

you've made a good start! Now take a break

Section 2

- The Putnams spy witchcraft.
- Mr. Parris protests in vain.
- Mrs. Putnam's dead babies.
- Abigail makes the girls agree on their story.

"IT IS SURELY A STROKE OF HELL UPON YOU"

Abigail and Mr. Parris are interrupted by the arrival of a wealthy married couple, the Putnams. Mrs. Putnam wants to know how high Betty flew over Ingersoll's barn. (In popular superstition, witches are able to fly.) The Putnams' own daughter, Ruth, is unconscious, although walking around with her eyes open. *"Her soul is taken, surely,"* cries Ann Putnam about Betty. The Putnams are determined to impose their own interpretation on events. With them, the witch-hunting hysteria enters the play. Mr. Putnam is less excited, but equally certain that there is witchcraft. Reverend Parris begs Mr. Putnam not to spread *so disastrous a charge* against him. His pleas will become increasingly feeble, as the Putnams show their contempt by interrupting and contradicting him. Both of them are embittered by personal grievances.

MRS. PUTNAM'S DEAD BABIES

Ann Putnam tells the minister that she lost seven children soon after birth. Ruth has been *turning strange* over the past year. Fearing to lose her too—and apparently ignorant about adolescence—she sent her daughter to Tituba to find out who had murdered her babies, because *Tituba knows how to speak to the dead.* Ironically, this is one of only two examples of attempted witchcraft in the play. Ruth was *close to their little spirits,* but she cannot tell her mother because *some power of darkness would stop her mouth.* Mr. Parris is horrified. *"It is a formidable sin to conjure up the dead,"* he cries. Yet, he does not dare criticize the wife of such an important man too strongly. He is also more concerned that Abigail has lied to him.

His niece immediately puts the blame on Ruth and Tituba.
Mr. Putnam urges the minister to save himself by declaring
publicly that he has discovered witchcraft. Parris reluctantly
agrees to meet his visitors, but only to lead them in a psalm.
This persistent refusal to confront the situation removes his
last chance to control events. Meanwhile, Mercy Lewis, the
Putnams' servant, has arrived to visit Betty. She brings news
that Ruth has *improved a little*. This sends Mrs. Putnam
hurrying home, and when the adults have left, we hear what
really happened in the forest.

In contrast to her indecisive uncle, Abigail instantly takes
charge. She stops Mercy from striking Betty, but only in case
Mr. Parris returns, and brings her up to date. They are joined
by Mary Warren, panic-stricken because *the whole country's
talkin' witchcraft! "They'll be callin' us witches, Abby!"* Look
carefully at what the three girls say to each other. (*"What'll
we do? ... a grand peeping courage you have."*) ❻ What
do we learn about their relationship and attitudes toward
one another? The answer has a bearing on what happens to
Mary during the court scene in Act 3.

Abigail tries to awaken Betty with a mixture of reassurance
and threats. The girl recovers and makes a sudden dash to the
window, calling for her mother. When she tries to climb out
Abigail pulls her back. Betty accuses Abigail of another lie:
*"You drank blood, Abby, you didn't tell him that! ... You drank
a charm to kill John Proctor's wife!"*

This lets us know that Betty must have been pretending
to be unconscious, at least some of the time. The
second remark about the Proctors prompts a violent response
from Abigail. ❻ When was the previous reference? She hits
Betty across the face, saying, *"We danced. And Tituba
conjured Ruth Putnam's dead sisters. And that is all."*

Abigail's short, staccato sentences emphasize her willpower and determination. She utters fierce threats of
what will happen to the girls if they don't stick to her version
of events. At this point, Abigail is concentrating on her
own survival. In the meantime, Betty has collapsed back
on her bed. While Abigail tries to shake her awake, John
Proctor enters.

Consolidate what you've read

?   Pick out the earlier lines of dialogue that may have suggested what Betty says when she "wakes up."

?   Draw a Mind Map with Betty in the center. Around her place the characters we have met so far and summarize the reaction of each to her mysterious illness. (Make up your own icons or copy those used in this book.)

Take some time off before seeing how John and Abigail react to each other

Section 3

◆ John and Abigail.

"YOU LOVED ME, AND YOU LOVE ME YET"

Mary Warren, another 17-year-old, is the Proctors' servant. When John Proctor enters, he is displeased to find her there and orders her to return to her work. He threatens her with a beating. (We learn later that she already knows about the relationship between John and Abigail.) Mercy Lewis— *strangely titillated*—decides she must return to Ruth Putnam's bedside. She stays away for a few minutes, perhaps to give Abigail the chance to be alone with John, and returns at the end of their scene together.

Notice how many times John and Abigail touch during their conversation. Even before they begin to talk, Abigail's manner and way of looking at John reveal that she finds him intensely attractive. When the others exit, Abigail makes a provocative remark, and John replies with a *knowing smile*. John says he has come to find out the reason for all this talk of witchcraft. Abigail replies scornfully that Betty's illness resulted from the fright Mr. Parris gave them. John is amused and turns to go, but Abigail springs into his path, begging for a *soft word*. Miller's stage direction reads, *her concentrated desire destroys his smile.* ✪ In view of what John admits later, is he naive to be surprised by her reaction?

His emphatic refusal, *"No, no, Abby. That's done with,"* tells us exactly what has happened. For John the affair is over, but Abigail will not accept rejection. The conversation develops into a battle of wills, John protesting that he has never given her reason to hope, while Abigail struggles to make him admit that he still desires her. John feels guilty because he betrayed his wife, and perhaps because he is still attracted to Abigail. This affects his ability to deal with the situation. He denies he has stood at night below Abigail's window, and then admits *"I may have looked up."* He remains firm against her tears and entreaties. *"I will cut off my hand before I'll ever reach for you again. Wipe it out of mind. We never touched, Abby."* ✪ Is he trying to pretend the affair never happened?

Abigail is enraged by John's denial; she sneers at Elizabeth Proctor as a *cold, snivelling woman ... who is blackening my name in the village.* The criticism of his wife goads John into shaking Abigail. *"Do you look for a whippin'?"* he demands. The threat reminds us that in seducing the much younger Abigail, John has also abused his authority in the home. Abigail makes a passionate plea for understanding—perhaps her only truly honest speech in the whole play—ending with the words *"John pity me, pity me!"* Significantly, John does not deny the accusation *"You love me yet!"* John's firm rebuff arouses Abigail's potential for destruction. By the end of Act 1, she has changed from being a teenager escaping the consequences of a silly prank into someone far more dangerous.

Some questions about John and Abigail

? What does this scene add to our knowledge of Abigail?
? How much do you feel for her, and why?
? What do you think of the way John handles his meeting with Abigail?

now have a change of scene yourself!

Section 4

◆ Rebecca and Proctor try to calm the situation.
◆ Parris demands his rights ...
◆ ... and Putnam claims John's land.

"YOU MUST STAND STILL"

This intense conversation ends when Betty cries out, and Mr. Parris and the Putnams rush in to see what has happened. Two new characters appear, Rebecca Nurse and Giles Corey.

Rebecca's gentleness has a calming effect on Betty. She suggests a natural cause for both children's illness and advises Reverend Parris to avoid more arguing by sending Mr. Hall back as soon as he arrives. *"There is prodigious danger in the seeking of loose spirits. Let us rather blame ourselves."* Rebecca is referring to the arguing in the village, but the Putnams are obsessed by their own problems. Thomas protests that *the Putnam seed have peopled this province*, and his wife goes on linking present events with the death of her babies. *"You think it God's work you should never lose a child ... and I bury all but one?"* We see a dangerous thought being planted. Mr. Putnam commands the minister to start a witch-hunt as soon as Mr. Hale appears.

TENSIONS IN THE COMMUNITY

This leads to a confrontation between John Proctor and Mr. Putnam, who accuses John of not attending church on Sunday. He retorts, *"I have trouble enough without I come five mile to hear him preach only hellfire and bloody damnation."* Mr. Parris launches into bitter complaints against his parishioners. Most of this emerges as a personal quarrel with John. Rebecca tries to take the heat out of the situation, saying to John, *"You cannot break charity with your minister ... Clasp his hand, make your peace."*

Giles, who has supported John throughout the argument, now shows his impulsive and contradictory nature by openly admiring Mr. Parris's "iron." When John jokes about the old man's habit of going to the law, Giles becomes annoyed, but John good-humoredly asks for his help to drag home some wood. Mr. Putnam cries out that the land is his, and no one else has a right to cut wood there.

(The playwright is skillfully drawing our attention to the type of dispute that Thomas Putnam will exploit during the witch-hunt.) Giles and John brush aside his complaints. They are on the point of leaving when Mr. Hale enters the room.

Time for a recap

? Before reading about Mr. Hale's attempts to identify the witch, summarize the plot so far in 50 words (or less). Don't bother to explain who the characters are.

? What are the main sources of dispute in the community? Try to answer in images, rather than a list of words.

? How might such squabbles weaken people's resistance to witch-hunting hysteria?

before you meet Mr. Hale the witch-finder, take some time off

Section 5

- ◆ Enter Mr. Hale, the witch-finder.
- ◆ He examines Betty for signs of the Devil.
- ◆ Giles makes a fatal mistake.
- ◆ Mr. Hale questions Abigail.

"THE DEVIL IS PRECISE"

Mr. Hale, the minister from Beverly, carries a pile of books listing *all the invisible world, caught, defined and calculated*. This reminds us that the New England Puritans believed unquestioningly in the authority of written texts. Reverend Parris is overwhelmed. He introduces Hale to the people gathered around Betty's bed. John Proctor leaves them with a skeptical remark. He doesn't take the proceedings seriously, and wants no part in them. Giles stays on to ask *some few queer questions.*

Hale's words to Rebecca contrast painfully with his reluctance to stand up for her in Act 2, and he shows himself to be a bit of a boot-licker to the Putnams. However, the remark to Rebecca, *"You look as such a good soul should,"* hints at qualities that will later enable him to renounce his dogmatic beliefs. He sets out by urging caution. Unfortunately, he is impatient to try out his skills, and his audience is eager to accept whatever is suggested to them. He allows their hysteria to overcome his reason.

While looking into Betty's illness, Hale learns about the dancing in the forest, the death of Mrs. Putnam's babies, and the fact that she sent her daughter to conjure up their spirits. Notice that he does not criticize Ann Putnam's behavior. Rebecca Nurse, on the contrary, is revolted, and her main concern is the possible harm to Ruth Putnam. Shortly afterward, she leaves the room, her disapproval resented by everyone. Rebecca is the only person who tries to heal the divisions in the community. Her exit marks the disappearance of common sense and moderation from Salem.

Giles seizes his chance to question the minister. His wife reads *strange books.* It stops him from repeating his prayers. When she walks out of the house, he finds he can pray again. ✪ From what you have seen of Giles, can you suggest why he might be unable to pray when his wife is reading? Hale is distracted for a moment, but he wants to get back to his work. Notice how those he interrogates take up his suggestions. He asks Betty whether any person or creature afflicts her. (People believed the Devil could disguise himself.) Betty doesn't answer. Mr. Hale tries to exorcise the Devil in Latin.

When this, too, has no effect, he begins to question Abigail about the girls' activities in the forest. For a few moments Abigail gets away with evasive answers, but Hale is hot on the scent. He demands to know whether she called up the Devil. Running out of lies, the girl insists she *didn't see no Devil* and, in desperation, mentions Tituba. Hale sends for the slave. While they wait for her, Abigail makes a last frantic attempt to awaken Betty. She fails. This is probably the moment when she decides to sacrifice Tituba for her own protection.

Keeping Track

? What details associated with witchcraft does Mr. Hale mention in this section? Begin to list them in icon form, and keep a record of how Abigail makes use of them later. Clue—*a sudden cold wind.* See what others you can find.

? Giles's interruptions form one of the structural elements in the play and lead inevitably to his downfall. Draw a countdown clock for Giles, inserting each incident as it happens now and later in the play. (Incidents are listed at the end of Commentary.)

Time for a break before the witch-hunt begins

Section 6

♦ Abigail blames Tituba.
♦ Tituba admits she saw the Devil.
♦ Tituba names the witches.
♦ Abigail and the girls join in.

"YOU HAVE SENT YOUR SPIRIT OUT UPON THIS CHILD"

Mrs. Putnam enters with Tituba, and Abigail instantly cries out, *"She made me do it! She made Betty do it! She made me drink blood!"* Mr. Hale tells the slave, *"You have sent your spirit out upon this child."* In other words, after selling her soul to the Devil, Tituba can use her own invisible phantom to inflict physical injury on people.

Tituba reacts with shock and bewilderment, then is terrified into submission. Note how Mr. Hale doesn't try to establish basic facts before making a judgment. He assumes certain things are true. *"When did you compact with the Devil?"* he asks Tituba. He brushes aside her denial. Frightened or angry people are not likely to accept a natural explanation or blame themselves.

Mr. Hale is not an unkind man. He doesn't threaten Tituba with the whip or the noose, like Reverend Parris and Mr. Putnam. He is genuinely eager to save her soul. Unintentionally, he is responsible for the witch-hunt. He tells Tituba that she can free her soul from Satan if she names others as witches. *"Tituba, you are chosen to help us cleanse our village. So speak utterly."* Tituba knows that her life depends on giving Mr. Hale the information he wants. She accuses the two old women that Mr. Putnam has already named, poor, friendless, and slightly disreputable. Before she gives in completely, there is a grimly comic moment when Tituba describes what the Devil told her to do to her master. *"Mr. Parris mean man ... and he bid me rise out of my bed and cut your throat."* ❍ Is Tituba deliberately frightening Mr. Parris, or is she already succumbing to the hallucinations she experiences in jail (Act 4)?

ABIGAIL RISES TO THE OCCASION

Suddenly, Abigail cries out. She has realized that enthusiastic repentance is an even better way to remove suspicion than passing on the blame. *"I want to open myself! I want the light of God, I want the sweet love of Jesus!"* She adds another name: *"I saw Bridget Bishop with the Devil!"* Betty rises from her bed. She is fully awake. She *picks up the chant*, and in alternating chorus the two girls name eight more women they claim to have seen with the Devil. With Betty's "awakening," the witch-hunt has begun.

Try these questions

? During this act, is Betty conscious (a) all the time, or (b) only some of the time? If (a), why was she pretending? If (b), what caused her to be in this state? Remember, she did actually faint in the forest.

? Would it have made any difference if Rebecca Nurse had stayed in the room?

? Draw a diagram to illustrate the stages by which Tituba is forced to confess. Keep it handy to compare with what happens to other victims in Act 3.

? Who made the following remarks, and why? From memory—don't cheat!

"Aye, a dress. And I thought I saw—someone naked running through the trees!"

"The whole country's talking witchcraft! They'll be calling us witches, Abby!"

"You bid me tear the light out of my eyes? I will not, I cannot!"

"Take courage, you must give us all their names."

"How can you bear to see this child suffering?"

now you've met all the main characters except Elizabeth and Danforth, take a break

Act 2 *Eight days later, the common room in the Proctors' house*

Section 1

♦ A strained marriage.
♦ Bad news from Salem.
♦ Abigail is the cause of the Proctors' quarrel.

"THE MAGISTRATE SITS IN YOUR HEART THAT JUDGES YOU"

After the frenzied climax of Act 1, we find ourselves in the quiet setting of the Proctors' farmhouse five miles outside Salem. Before a word is spoken, a small domestic detail sums up how John's guilt has damaged his marriage. Furtively, he adds some salt to his supper and then praises Elizabeth's cooking. They discuss the work of the farm, treating each other very warily. At one point John gets up to kiss Elizabeth; he is disappointed when *she receives it.* ❂ Why is he disappointed?

When he has finished his meal, Elizabeth tells him that Mary Warren has disobeyed them by going into Salem. John is annoyed that Elizabeth hasn't been able to control Mary. She says that Mary is *like the daughter of a prince* since she became a court official.

Four judges from Boston are trying the people accused of witchcraft. They imprison anyone named by Abigail and her friends. Elizabeth urges John to denounce the girls as frauds; she reminds him that Abigail said their fits had nothing to do with witchcraft. John admits that he was alone with Abigail at the time. This contradicts his previous statement. Resenting the lie, Elizabeth turns away coldly, and John is annoyed that she still suspects him. Elizabeth replies, *"If it were not Abigail that you must go to hurt, would you falter now?"*

John becomes even angrier and tells her to *Learn charity.* ❂ What does he mean by this? When she protests that she thinks him a good man, and that his own conscience judges him, John comments bitterly, *"Your justice would freeze beer!"*

?   How accurate is Abigail's description of Elizabeth: *a cold, snivelling woman*?

?   Reread the passage *"I think we'll see green fields soon ... Massachusetts is a beauty in the spring!"* Pick out phrases showing John's enjoyment of his physical senses.

?   How does this fit in with Abigail's description of him as *no wintry man*?

?   What details in the same passage indicate that Elizabeth is unable—or unwilling—to respond in the same way?

give yourself a break before hearing the news that Mary brings back from Salem

Section 2

◆ Mary brings news from the court.
◆ "She wants me dead, John."

"I HEAR A VOICE, A SCREAMIN' VOICE, AND IT WERE MY VOICE"

When Mary Warren returns home, her strange behavior quells John's anger. She is deeply affected by her experience in court. Tearful and exhausted, she says, *"We must all love each other now,"* and presents Elizabeth with a "poppet"—a rag doll—which she made while sitting through the trials. She tells the Proctors that 39 people are now in jail. Goody Osburn is to be hanged. Sarah Good will live because she confessed. Though shocked, John and Elizabeth can hardly believe anyone would take such accusations seriously. Mary claims that Sarah Good *near to choked us all to death.*

Mary's speech (*"I never knew it ... she done to me!"*) vividly describes the onset of hysteria. She relives the sensations she felt in court—*misty coldness ... a clamp round my neck.*

She told the judge that Sarah Good always mumbled when she turned her away from the Proctors' door. *"She may mumble if she's hungry,"* John comments scornfully. Sarah said she was not cursing Mary, but reciting the Commandments. Yet she could not repeat a single one. Mary concludes, *"It's hard proof, hard as rock, the judges said."*

John orders Mary not to go to court again. When she defies him, he takes down his whip. Mary points at Elizabeth. *"I saved her life today!"* she cries. We know the accusation must have come from Abigail. John lowers the whip. Mary regains her self-confidence and demands to be treated with more respect. She refuses to go to bed. When John leaves her the choice, she goes upstairs after all.

The few comic moments in the play, like this example, all emphasize the deepening horror of the situation. John and Elizabeth, both strong characters, are at the mercy of a weak, impressionable girl. ✪ What is the source of Mary's power over them?

"SHE WANTS ME DEAD, JOHN"

After Mary goes to bed, the Proctors discuss what to do. Elizabeth is sure that Abigail intends to get her hanged so she may marry John herself. He offers to do what his wife has already suggested—tell Cheever about Abigail's admission of fraud. Elizabeth thinks he must do more. She is trembling with fear. Braving her husband's anger, she begs him to convince Abigail she is deceiving herself. *"You have a faulty understanding of young girls. ... Go and tell her she's a whore. Whatever promise she may sense—break it, John, break it."*

John's reaction exposes a web of complex emotions. He tells Elizabeth she does not understand his shame, and is too obsessed with a moment of sheer physical lust. *"The promise that a stallion gives a mare I gave that girl!"* ✪ When was the word *stallion* used before? He insists he is honest—that he gave Abigail no promises for the future. He is too angry to reflect that he may have misled her unintentionally. Neither of the Proctors realizes that Abigail will not take no for an answer. Elizabeth accuses John of still being attracted to Abigail. At the height of their quarrel, Mr. Hale enters.

How well have you understood?

? Suggest what Elizabeth might have been about to say when Mary cut her short, "*Oh, Mary, Mary, surely you …*"

? Do you agree with Elizabeth, "*She has an arrow in you yet?*"

? Draw a seesaw as below. On its ends, list what links John to Elizabeth, and to Abigail.

Take a break, before the outside world breaks into the Proctors' home

Section 3

◆ Mr. Hale examines the Proctors.
◆ Why John dislikes Mr. Parris.
◆ The seventh Commandment.
◆ John says the girls are frauds.
◆ Martha and Rebecca have been arrested.

"MR. PROCTOR, THAT IS NOT FOR YOU TO DECIDE"

Mr. Hale's visit demonstrates the power of the Church in Salem. He is going from house to house *to draw a clear opinion of them that come accused before the court.* He is embarrassed at having to cross-examine respectable families, but still unshakably convinced that his interpretation of events is correct. *The powers of the dark are gathered in monstrous attack upon this village.* He assures the Proctors that Rebecca Nurse is safe; she is only *mentioned somewhat.* He disagrees with John that it is impossible for such a good woman to be in league with the Devil, but he adds, *"She is far from accused, and I know she will not be."* ✪ What does this remark tell us about Mr. Hale's state of mind?

The minister questions John about his absence from church. John explains that Elizabeth was sick that winter and he had prayed at home, but Hale is not satisfied. John reveals his strong dislike of Parris, complaining that he has forced his congregation to pay for golden candlesticks for the meetinghouse, and tells Hale he sees *no light of God in that man.* Elizabeth realizes what a bad impression her husband is making, and says tactfully, *"Maybe, we have been too hard with Mr. Parris."*

Hale asks the Proctors whether they know their Commandments. ✪ When were the Commandments mentioned before in this act? They both say "Yes," and he asks John to repeat them. ✪ Why does he choose John and not Elizabeth? John sticks on the seventh, *Thou shalt not commit adultery,* and his wife prompts him. When John tries to pass it off with a joke, the minister rebukes him sternly. *"Theology, sir, is a fortress; no crack in a fortress may be accounted small."*

"THE CHILDREN'S SICKNESS HAD NAUGHT TO DO WITH WITCHCRAFT"

Mr. Hale is on the point of leaving, unable to hide his misgivings. Elizabeth prods John into telling him that the girls' behavior has a natural explanation. *"Mr. Parris discovered them sportin' in the woods. They were startled and took sick."* Mr. Hale is startled; why wasn't he told this before? John cannot give him the true reason, so he gives an unconvincing answer.

Mr. Hale points out that everyone he has examined has *confessed to dealing with the Devil.* *"And why not, if they must hang for denyin' it?"* retorts John.

Mr. Hale half-thinks this too, but he suppresses the thought. He extracts a promise that John will repeat his evidence in court and examines both Proctors on their belief in witches. The minister's questioning outrages Elizabeth. She takes it as a criticism of her Christian faith, and cries out, *"Question Abigail Williams about the Gospel, not myself!"* John springs to his wife's defense.

As Hale makes a second attempt to leave, Giles Corey arrives with Francis Nurse. Their wives have been arrested. Note that the accusations have now spread outside the circle of girls. Francis pleads with Mr. Hale to speak up for the women. To everyone else, the arrest of Rebecca proves that the accusations are fraudulent. Mr. Hale's reaction is, *"If Rebecca Nurse be tainted, then nothing's left to stop the whole green world from burning. ... Rest upon the justice of the court ... We dare not quail to follow wherever the accusing finger points!"*

Pause here for questions

?   Why do you think Elizabeth manages to keep calm until the end of Mr. Hale's visit, and then seems to go out of her way to provoke him?

?   Mr. Hale is kinder than most of the court officials. Does this make us more or less apprehensive for the Proctors, and why?

be kind to yourself—relax for a while!

Section 4

◆ Cheever tries to arrest Elizabeth.
◆ Mary explains about the poppet.
◆ Elizabeth gives herself up.

"I HAVE A WARRANT FOR YOUR WIFE"

While Giles describes why his wife was arrested, Ezekiel Cheever and Marshal Herrick enter. They are the court's arresting officers, and their arrival finally destroys John Proctor's attempts to shut out the outside world. Cheever has a warrant to arrest Elizabeth. He asks whether there are any "poppets" in the house. His eyes fall on Mary's present, which Elizabeth has put up on the mantlepiece. She hands over the doll, and Cheever tries to arrest her without explaining its significance. While Elizabeth goes to get Mary, Cheever becomes very excited when he discovers a needle under the doll's skirt.

He explains that during supper that evening, Abigail screamed and fell to the floor. Mr. Parris drew out a needle buried two inches deep in her body. Abigail claimed that Elizabeth's invisible spirit had pushed it in. *"Why, she done it herself!"* cries John. ✪ What else does this incident tell us about Abigail?

At this point, Elizabeth returns with Mary Warren, who admits that she sewed the doll in court and tucked the needle in there herself. Hale realizes that if Mary is speaking the truth, Abigail must be plotting to murder Elizabeth. He asks Mary if someone is putting words into her mouth. Mary tells him that Abigail sat beside her while she sewed.

John rips up the Deputy-Governor's warrant and orders Cheever to leave. He turns savagely on Hale as well. *"Why do you never wonder if Parris be innocent, or Abigail? ... This warrant's vengeance! I'll not give my wife to vengeance!"* When Hale insists *The court is just*, John accuses him of acting like Pontius Pilate. ✪ What does he mean?

Elizabeth resolves the situation: *"John, I think I must go with them."* She has regained her self-control and gives instructions to Mary for running the house in her absence. Then she lets the court officials take her away. The arrests affected more than the victims; this poignant episode brings home the devastation they inflicted on whole families. There is a final outburst from John when he hears the clank of chains; he rushes out to protest and is dragged back by Herrick and two deputies. Typical of all underlings in authoritarian regimes, Herrick protests that he is only doing his duty.

When the officials have left, John orders Hale from his house. The minister urges John not to *lay the cause to the vengeance of a little girl.* ◯ What vengeance does Hale mean? Is it different from John's vengeance? He urges the three men to reflect whether some great sin committed in the village *may have drawn such thundering wrath.* John asks Giles and Francis to go away. *He has been reached by Hale's words.* ◯ What does this mean?

After his friends have left, John tells Mary that she must come to court to let everyone know the truth about the poppet. Mary protests that she is terrified of Abigail. *"She'll kill me for sayin' that! Abby'll charge lechery on you, Mr. Proctor!"* John is taken aback that Mary knows about their affair, but thrusts his hesitation aside. *"Good ... We will slide together into our pit, and you will tell what you know."* He throws Mary to the floor; she continues to sob, *"I cannot, I cannot,"* as the curtain falls.

Test yourself

? What do you think John intends to do when he says he will *fall like an ocean on that court*?

? Draw a Mind Map showing the charges on which Rebecca, Martha, and Elizabeth have been arrested. Include also those who have accused them, and what you consider the true motives behind the accusations.

? There are two moments when Mr. Hale's language becomes very elaborate. Can you find them and say why he starts to talk in this way?

The next act is complicated—prepare for it with a long break to refresh yourself

Act 3 *The vestry room of the Salem meetinghouse, two weeks later*

Section 1

◆ Giles tries to save his wife.
◆ Francis accuses the girls of fraud.

"YOU'RE HEARING LIES, LIES!"

Act 3 begins with the consequences of Giles's rash complaint about his wife. ✪ What did he say about her to Mr. Hale? Offstage, Martha denies that she is a witch, and Giles's interruptions throw the court into an uproar. Herrick ejects him into the vestry room. Hathorne, a junior judge, enters and rebukes Giles. When Deputy-Governor Danforth appears, followed by Cheever and Parris, the room falls silent. Danforth is president of the court. More intelligent and thoughtful than the other officials, he seems touched by Giles's grief. Nevertheless, he is completely inflexible. He says that Giles's evidence must be written down.

"WE HAVE PROOF FOR YOUR EYES"

Danforth is equally firm with Francis Nurse when he claims that the girls are frauds. He tries to crush Francis with a reminder that 400 people are in jail on his signature and 72 waiting to be hanged.

Test yourself

? What have you learned about the procedures of the court so far?
? What differences in attitude have you noticed between the two judges?
? What do you think the people in the court are *roaring* about?

There's a long trial ahead—Take a break

Section 2

- ◆ John brings Mary to court.
- ◆ Danforth suspects John's motives.
- ◆ "She is saved ... will you drop this charge?"
- ◆ Those who signed will be arrested.

"IT WERE PRETENCE, SIR"

Giles reenters with John Proctor and Mary Warren. Mary is too overcome to talk, so John says on her behalf that the girls *never saw no spirits.* ✪ Why is Mr. Parris, *on seeing her, in shock*? Danforth refuses to accept Mary's signed deposition when John tries to hand it over. (Compare this with his treatment of Giles.) He tells John, *"The entire contention of the state in these trials is that the voice of Heaven is speaking through the children."* Danforth is baffled that Mary—now acting for herself—continues to assert that she and the rest of the girls were pretending. Before beginning his investigation, he warns John, *"We burn a hot fire here; it melts down all concealment."* This is the crucible of the title, but the truth that emerges at the end of the play is not Judge Danforth's truth.

Danforth thinks that in order to save Elizabeth, John has told Mary what to tell the court. Cheever and Mr. Parris try to discredit John; he has ripped up the court warrant, is seldom seen in Church, and he plows on Sunday. *"I cannot think you may judge the man on such evidence,"* protests Mr. Hale. ✪ What difference do you see in his attitude now? Danforth assures the minister that such details do not influence him, but he does not accept that the girls have deceived him. *"I have seen people choked before my eyes by spirits ... stuck by pins and slashed by daggers."*

Danforth reveals that Elizabeth claims to be pregnant. If she is telling the truth, she will not hang for another year at least. (It is unlawful to kill an unborn child.) John assures the judge, *"That woman will never lie, Mr. Danforth"*—a statement that will have terrible consequences. Contrary to the judge's expectation, John refuses to withdraw the charge of fraud as long as his friends' wives are in danger. This is John's first step toward accepting social responsibility. Danforth gives in, and orders a court recess while he examines John's papers.

First, John hands over a list of 91 people who declare their good opinion of the three wives—Rebecca, Elizabeth, and Martha. Parris and Hathorne, the junior judge, urge Mr. Danforth to arrest them for questioning. Despite Francis's protest that he has guaranteed their safety, Danforth agrees. If these people are innocent, they have nothing to fear.

Try these three questions before going on

?   Do you think Mary had really been ill the previous week?

?   Why does Danforth show alarm as well as surprise when Proctor tells him *Mary never saw no spirits*?

?   Why is Parris so eager to prove that witchcraft has taken place in the village when he tried so hard to deny it in Act 1?

things go from bad to worse; fortify yourself with a break before continuing

Section 3

◆ Giles accuses Putnam.
◆ Mr. Hale begins to protest.
◆ John presents Mary's deposition.
◆ Danforth sends for the children.
◆ He questions Mary.

"I WILL NOT GIVE YOU NO NAME"

Danforth is now ready to look at Mary's deposition; but Giles is eager for the judge to first look at his own. This interruption is typical of Giles's impetuous nature; it also keeps up the tension as we wait for Mary's cross-examination. What soon becomes apparent is that Giles and John are no match for the ruthless judge.

Danforth reads the deposition and compliments Giles on his legal skill. The old man rambles on about past disputes with his neighbors until Thomas Putnam enters. Giles has alleged that Putnam ordered his daughter to denounce George Jacobs as a witch. (He is the first male witch to be accused.) *"I have it from an honest man who heard Putnam say it! The day his daughter cried out on Jacobs, he said she'd given him a fair gift of land."* ✪ When was Putnam's habit of acquiring his neighbors' land mentioned before? Putnam says this is a lie. Asked to give the name of his informant, Giles refuses. Danforth threatens to arrest him, and he smartly points out that he cannot be arrested during a hearing. Danforth promptly declares that the court is now in session.

Proctor points out that Giles had the story in confidence; Hale also pleads with Danforth: *"There is a prodigious fear of this court in the country."* Danforth overrules him. *"No uncorrupted man may fear this court"*—an approach he will maintain rigidly throughout the play. He arrests Giles for contempt of court.

"I THINKS THIS GOES TO THE HEART OF THE MATTER"

At last John has a chance to present Mary's evidence. *He is speaking reasonably, restraining all his fears.* Hale attempts to halt the proceedings. *"A claim so weighty cannot be argued by a farmer ... let him come again with a lawyer. ... I have signed seventy-two death warrants ... I dare not take a life without there be proof ... immaculate."* We learn that Rebecca has been condemned to death. ✪ Why is Hale so agitated? Is he concerned to see justice done, or does he just want to save his reputation?

Judge Danforth gently mocks the minister. *"For a man of such terrible learning you are most bewildered."* He explains how he intends to proceed. Since witchcraft is an invisible crime, there can be no witnesses for the defense, so the court must rely on the witch's victims for evidence. He is about to consider their truthfulness.

For a few tense moments, the others wait while Danforth reads Mary's deposition. He asks Cheever to bring the girls before him, and starts to question Mary. At first she holds up well, despite her fear. She rejects the suggestion that John Proctor threatened her. Even when Danforth threatens her with jail, she perseveres in her story. The door opens to let in Betty, Mercy, Susanna, and Abigail.

Consider these points

? Was it reasonable for Giles to expect the judge to accept his allegation against Thomas Putnam?

? Fill in the rest of your countdown clock for Giles.

? Look at Judge Danforth's speech: *"Mr. Hale, believe me … Have I not?"* Are his principles fair and just? Give reasons for your answer.

now break off for a while before hearing Abigail's evidence

Section 4

◆ Abigail lies about the poppet.
◆ John accuses her.
◆ Mary cannot faint.
◆ Is Abigail cornered?

ABIGAIL CONTRADICTS MARY

Judge Danforth solemnly warns the girls that the Bible damns all liars as well as those who practice witchcraft. If Satan is using Mary to distract the court, she will hang; if not, a quick confession will bring them lighter punishment. Is there any truth in Mary's story, he asks Abigail. *"No, sir,"* she replies, with impressive simplicity. Mary's account of the poppet is false, and Elizabeth Proctor always kept dolls in her house. In support of her lies, Parris and Hathorne reach such heights of absurdity that John cries out, *"There might also be a dragon with five heads in my house, but no one has ever seen it."*

"I CANNOT FAINT NOW, SIR"

Danforth reminds Proctor that he is charging Abigail with a plot to murder. John is still reluctant to disclose why Abigail hates his wife. He describes her unseemly behavior in church and the expeditions into the forest. In a Puritan community, these are serious matters. Danforth's view of Abigail begins to change, so Hathorne tries to bully Mary into contradicting herself. If she was only pretending to faint, let her show them how she did it. Of course, Mary cannot. Hathorne demands, *"How could you think you saw them* [spirits] *unless you saw them?"* Mary is confused, but she has a dim insight into the truth. She stammers, *"I heard the other girls screaming, and you, Your Honour, you seemed to believe them ... It were only sport in the beginning ... but then the whole world cried spirits, spirits ... ."*

Danforth is impressed by Mary's words. He is the only person who grasps—very briefly—that the girls' behavior results neither from demonic possession nor totally deliberate pretense. For the first and only time, he shows some doubt about the reality of satanic possession in Salem. He asks Abigail, *"Is it possible, child, that the spirits you have seen are illusion only?"*

This is the turning point of the play. Abigail is disconcerted and unable to give a satisfactory answer. This time her bold lies will not be enough; she will suffer serious consequences if she is discredited. Everything depends on quick thinking. She puts on a show of indignation. *"I have been near to murdered every day ... and this is my reward? To be mistrusted, denied ..."* So convincing is she that Danforth weakens. Abigail follows up her advantage by threatening him: *"Think you be so mighty that the power of Hell may not turn your wits?"*

Test yourself

? Compare Mary's speech in this section (*"I—I cannot tell how ... but I did not"*) with her reasons for accusing Sarah Good (*"I never knew it—everything she done to me,"* Act 2). Reread the section on hysteria. This will help to explain what happens next.

? Why is Mary unable to faint?

?   Find some earlier examples of Abigail's ability to defend herself by going on the attack.

?   How do you suppose Abigail feels toward John Proctor now?

The tension is mounting—take a deep breath and relax for a while!

Section 5

◆ The cold wind returns.
◆ John confesses his adultery.
◆ Danforth sends for Elizabeth.
◆ Her first lie.

"A WIND, A COLD WIND HAS COME"

Mary's inability to faint has given Abigail a brilliant idea. She begins to shiver and cry out, as though controlled by an external power. The other girls echo her: *"I freeze, I freeze!"* Danforth asks Mary *"Do you witch her ... do you send your spirit out?"* As the hysteria rises, he is *himself entered and engaged by Abigail.* Mary starts to run in terror, but John catches her. She begs him to let her go. Enraged at Abigail's victory, John springs forward to grab her by the hair. *"Whore! Whore!"* he shouts.

JOHN CONFESSES

There are astonished cries and questions; the girls are instantly silent. Ashamed and trembling, John confesses, *"I have known her, sir. I have known her."* Danforth forces him to give the details of his sexual encounter with Abigail. John can hardly speak; he knows that Elizabeth was right: He did raise Abigail's hopes. *"She thinks to dance with me on my wife's grave! And well she might ... I lusted, and there is a promise in such sweat."* John's despair and shame are too convincing to be ignored.

Danforth invites Abigail to deny the accusation. She threatens him again and tries to leave the room, but Danforth orders her to remain. He sends Parris to get Elizabeth. John repeats that his wife would never tell a lie and that she put Abigail out of the house for *harlotry*.

"SHE HAS SPOKEN. REMOVE HER!"

When Elizabeth enters, Danforth tells her to look at no one but himself. He has already ordered John and Abigail to turn their backs. He asks Elizabeth why she dismissed Abigail. Elizabeth is in an agonizing dilemma. She does not want to besmirch her husband's name; yet lying is a sin. She has no idea what John has said, and can only go on what has happened before. Uncertainly, she replies, *"She— dissatisfied me. And my husband."* Danforth presses her for a reason. With great unwillingness she admits, *"I came to think he fancied her."* So she had put Abigail out of the house. Danforth bluntly asks, *"Is your husband a lecher?"* Elizabeth replies, *"No, sir."* The judge immediately tells Herrick to remove her.

As she leaves the room, John cries out, *"I have confessed it!"* Mr. Hale speaks up in a futile attempt to save the situation. Danforth will not listen. He dismisses John's confession as a calculated lie, and insists that Elizabeth has told the truth. Hale persists: *"It is a natural lie to tell ... call back his wife. ... This girl has always struck me as false!"*

Test yourself

? Why is Danforth so quick to send Elizabeth away?

? John is mistaken in thinking Elizabeth will disclose his adultery in public. Why do you suppose he makes this error in judgment?

? If Elizabeth is willing to compromise her principles to help John, what does this tell us about Elizabeth herself, and her attitude toward John?

Take some time off before this act advances to its terrifying climax

Section 6

◆ Abigail sees a yellow bird.
◆ The girls terrify Mary.
◆ She returns to Abigail.
◆ John is arrested.

ABIGAIL'S TRIUMPH

This powerful scene performs a double function. We meet the full force of Abigail's ruthless personality. In addition, the band of hysterical adolescents symbolizes a more general fear that has paralyzed the adult community.

Abigail reacts swiftly to Hale's challenge. She looks up and screams that Mary is a yellow bird perched on the roof beam; the girls follow her lead. Hysteria sweeps around the room, engulfing everyone except John and Mr. Hale. Abigail pleads with the bird not to attack her face. Mary is too shocked to be afraid. *"She sees nothin'*," she protests angrily, and Abigail tries a new trick. Whenever Mary speaks, Abigail and the girls repeat her words. The relentless game goes on until Danforth himself is *growing hysterical*, and Mary is reduced to whimpering horror.

Abigail puts on more pressure; the "bird" swoops down on the screaming girls and they run across the room. Mary screams with them, louder and louder, until she goes into a fit that silences everyone. When John moves nearer, she backs away, calling him *the Devil's man*. She accuses him of forcing her to sign the deposition. *"I'll murder you,"* he says, *"if my wife hangs! We must go and overthrow the court."* She rushes sobbing to Abigail, who draws her into her arms.

John is speechless with anger. Danforth demands John's confession that he has sold himself to Satan. John breaks into a passionate denunciation of all who have allowed this corruption to flourish, *"Them that have quailed ... as I have quailed ... and ... you when you know ... that this be fraud ... we will burn together!"* Danforth orders Marshall Herrick to take John and Giles to jail, and Hale walks out in disgust. *"I denounce these proceedings, I quit this court!"* Now he has to grapple with his conscience, knowing that he has sent innocent people to their death.

Final questions

? Do you think that Abigail remains in control of herself throughout, or is she ever caught up in the hysteria?

? How does John's attitude and behavior in this act differ from what we saw in Act 2?

? Would it have made any difference if John had confessed his adultery earlier?

? How has Mr. Hale changed since Act 2?

? Draw a diagram to show how the images of cold and heat are used in this act.

? One of the best ways of grasping a complicated series of events is to turn them into rhyming couplets and to learn them by heart. It doesn't matter how bad your verses are—the rhymes will have an amazing effect on your recall. Here is a sample for Act 3. Finish it yourself! If you find this helpful, use it for the other acts of the play.

> Giles and Francis fear their wives will die;
> Mary says she told a lie.
> "If I free your wife, will you let this go?"
> Danforth asks John, and he says "No!"
> Giles claims Putnam is naming witches
> To grab more land and increase his riches.
> Mary confesses, but her spirits fail
> When her ex-friends enter with Abigail ...

Stretch your legs before a prison visit

Act 4 A cell in the Salem jail, that fall

Section 1

◆ Tituba and Sarah Good in jail.
◆ Mr. Parris wants to postpone the executions.

"THE PROPER MORNING TO FLY INTO HELL"

Act 4 takes us back to the dominant personal theme of the play: How can someone achieve moral honesty? It takes place in the Salem jail, several months after John's arrest. Seven prisoners are to be hanged that morning, including Rebecca, John, and Martha Corey. The room is dark and cold, the time almost morning. Sara Good and Tituba are waiting for the Devil to take them to Barbados. Marshal Herrick enters to clear the room for Reverend Parris and the two judges. When he tries to remove the prisoners, Tituba rushes to the window, where she mistakes a cow bellowing outside for the Devil. Herrick pushes the two women offstage to another cell. This opening scene rounds off the fate of two minor characters. The stray cows are mentioned again, underlining the social disruption caused by the witch-hunt. Moreover, the almost farcical tone releases the tension created at the end of Act 3, and provides a base from which the play can soar to its final climax.

"I WOULD POSTPONE THESE HANGIN'S FOR A TIME"

Danforth and Hathorne arrive first. The senior judge learns with anger that Mr. Parris has allowed Reverend Hale to pray with the prisoners. When Parris arrives, he explains that Hale is trying to make them confess and save their lives. ❷ Does this surprise you? However, Parris has summoned the judges to tell them that Abigail and Mercy Lewis have been missing for three nights. They have run away in case the rebellion at Andover spreads to Salem. Abigail has helped herself to the money in her uncle's strongbox. *"Thirty-one pound is gone.*

I am penniless," sobs Reverend Parris. Danforth is exasperated. *"Mr. Parris, you are a brainless man!"* He is deeply worried, but does not voice his thoughts. ❸ Why does the news make him anxious?

Parris argues that the prisoners executed so far had bad reputations, whereas John Proctor and Rebecca Nurse *have great weight yet in the town.* He fears there may be a riot and begs the judges to postpone the hangings until Hale has persuaded at least one person to confess. One admission would justify the hangings. *"That confession surely damns all the others in the public eye."* He has no concern for the victims' souls, much less their safety. Danforth refuses a postponement; he offers to work on the prisoners himself. We learn that they will be executed as soon as the sun rises. Parris reveals the real source of his terror—his life has been threatened. *"You cannot hang this sort. There is danger for me."*

Try these questions

? On what other occasion was Reverend Parris anxious to save himself?
? Does Danforth still believe that *the voice of Heaven* (Act 3) speaks through Abigail? If not, why does her disappearance have so little effect on his actions?

Take a short break now before meeting the prisoners

Section 2

◆ Mr. Hale and Judge Danforth agree to use Elizabeth.
◆ Mr. Hale begs Elizabeth to make John confess.

"THEM THAT WILL NOT CONFESS WILL HANG"

Mr. Hale enters and tells Danforth, *"You must pardon them. They will not budge."* The judge replies, *"I cannot pardon these when twelve are already hanged for the same crime. It is not just."* ✪ "Just" to whom? A long speech explains his reasons. *"Reprieve or pardon casts doubt upon the guilt of them that died till now."* Nothing must be allowed to melt the resolution of the statute. He cannot alter God's law to avoid retaliation.

Still convinced that he is in the right, Danforth naturally thinks that the end justifies the means and has no qualms about propping up God's law with mental torture. He wonders whether seeing his wife might soften John Proctor. ✪ Why does Danforth say, *"His wife must be well on with child now"*?

The judge orders Herrick to bring the Proctors to him. While they wait, Hale asks the judge to put off the executions for a week. Like Parris, he fears civil unrest. He has seen *"orphans wandering from house to house ... abandoned cattle ... on the highroads. ... You wonder yet if rebellion's spoke? Better you should marvel how they do not burn your province!"* Hale is weighed down by guilt for his part in starting the witch-hunt. The only way he can help the victims is to persuade them to lie.

"THAT BE THE DEVIL'S ARGUMENT"

As so often, Miller interrupts a moment of high tension by bringing on another character. Just as Hale cries out, *'Can you not see the blood on my head!'* Elizabeth enters. Danforth is *uncertain how to plead*, so he turns to Hale. The minister launches into a high-flown speech, ending with these words, *"Prevail upon your husband to confess. Let him give his lie."* ✪ Why does Hale take so long to get to the point? Why does he talk so much about himself, and why does he use such elaborate language?

Elizabeth responds to Mr. Hale's words by calling them *the Devil's argument*. ✪ Explain what she means. Judge Danforth takes over and tries to bully her into agreement. When she remains silent, he tells her that her *dry eyes* prove that she has sold herself to Satan. He orders her to be taken away. At this, Elizabeth asks to speak to her husband, but refuses to promise she will *plead for his confession*. John Proctor is brought in.

He is unkempt and filthy, vastly changed from when we last saw him. The others go out of the cell, leaving John and Elizabeth alone together.

Test yourself

? Is Hale motivated by genuine concern for others, or is he only trying to cope with his feelings of guilt?

? Why did Elizabeth ask to speak to John? What do you think she meant to say to him?

? On what kinds of occasions do people take a long time to get to the point of what they really want to say?

? Was Hale right to ask the prisoners to confess? Would you have done the same in his place?

what will Elizabeth say to John? Find out after the break.

Section 3

◆ Elizabeth refuses to influence her husband.

"IT IS NOT MY SOUL, JOHN, IT IS YOURS"

Think back to the last time Elizabeth and John were alone together. They were leading an ordinary family life in peaceful surroundings, but they were quarreling over John's affair with Abigail. ✪ What is the contrast in their present circumstances and attitude toward each other?

John asks about their unborn child and the three boys. Elizabeth describes what has happened during the past three months. More than a hundred people have confessed to avoid hanging. Giles Corey refused to plead "guilty" or "not guilty" and was crushed to death under a pile of stones. By refusing a trial, he made sure his sons would inherit his farm. John finds the news *a thread to weave into his agony.* ✪ What does this mean, besides his grief at Giles's death?

John Proctor is looking for a reason to do what he longs to do—save his life and be reunited with his family. *"I have been thinking I would confess to them, Elizabeth. What say you?"* Elizabeth admits *"I want you living, John. That's sure,"* but she refuses to advise him. John sees himself as a fraud who cannot *mount the gibbet like a saint.* He has not confessed so far, Elizabeth replies. *"That speak goodness in you."* John argues that only those who have never lied can die for the truth. By dying out of sheer pride, he, on the contrary, will win no credit with God, and his children will become beggars because the land will be auctioned.

Elizabeth's great strength of character is shown in her refusal to take the easy way out. John wants her to decide for him, because he still cannot cope with his sense of guilt. Elizabeth accepts the hard truth that if she does so, John will never be free of shame. *"It come to naught that I should forgive you, if you'll not forgive yourself ... Whatever you will do, it is a good man does it."* She says that she must share the blame for his adultery with Abigail: *"It needs a cold wife to prompt lechery."* As Judge Hathorne enters, she asks John to forgive her and implores him, *"Let none be your judge."*

Test yourself

? What details in this scene convey the intense emotion between John and Elizabeth?

? How does Giles's death fit in with what you know about him already?

? What previous conversation should we recall when Elizabeth says, *"John, it come to naught ... forgive yourself?"*

Take a break, and then see what John decides to do

Section 4

♦ John confesses to save his life.
♦ He redeems his name.

"I WANT MY LIFE"

John will not use the word "confess" to Hathorne. He says only *"I want my life."* The judge rushes out to spread the news, while Elizabeth weeps *in terror.* ✪ What is she afraid of? When Hathorne shouts *"Proctor will confess!"* John reacts with shame and self-hatred. He justifies his decision with the arguments he used before. Elizabeth does not answer when he asks if she would do the same.

Judge Danforth enters with Parris, Hale, and the court officials. John protests when he learns that they will write down his confession and display it on the church door. Nevertheless, he is ready to pretend that he saw the Devil and bound himself to his service.

Danforth then makes his great mistake. He has Rebecca Nurse brought in, hoping that John's example will encourage her to confess. Rebecca is hardly able to walk. She is astonished at John's action, and refuses to confess. *"It is a lie; how may I damn myself? I cannot, I cannot."* Danforth inquires whether John has ever seen Rebecca with the Devil. John says *"No."* The judge goes through the names on his sheet, repeating his question, and always receiving the same answer. Mixing threats and arguments, Danforth warns John that he must prove the "whiteness" of his soul by revealing the names of those he saw with the Devil. Otherwise, he will hang.

"YOU WILL NOT USE ME"

In the last scene, John Proctor at last sees clearly what he must do to regain his integrity. Danforth is highly dissatisfied with his answers, but it is already daylight and time for the executions. Cheever has written down John's confession. The two ministers urge Judge Danforth to be satisfied with what he has heard and allow John to sign the paper. Danforth reluctantly agrees. ✪ There are two very different motives behind the ministers' wish to conclude proceedings. What are they? After some hesitation, John puts his name on the paper, but he refuses to hand it over. *"I have confessed myself! ... God does not need my name nailed upon the church!"* How can he raise his children if everyone knows that he has betrayed his friends? He has not betrayed them, counters Danforth, meaning that he has refused to accuse them. Surely, he argues, it is the same whether people see the signed confession or hear from himself that John signed it.

"No, it is not the same!" John cries. He adds, *"I have given you my soul; leave me my name!"* Pressed by Danforth to explain, John at last realizes how false his position is. There is no way he can compromise; whether the confession becomes public or not, it will destroy both his reputation and, more important, the true core and identity of the man who is John Proctor. He must die to preserve his name.

John tears up the paper, amid protests from Parris and Hale. He tells them: *"Now I do think I see some shred of goodness in John Proctor. Not enough to weave a banner with, but white enough to keep it from such dogs."* Elizabeth weeps, but does not try to stop him. John exhorts her not to give them the pleasure of seeing her tears. He gives her a passionate farewell kiss, and then supports Rebecca as they are taken out of the room to be hanged.

There is a drumroll outside; Elizabeth turns to the window. Parris and Hale beg her to intervene before it is too late. She answers them with the last words of the play, *"He have his goodness now. God forbid I take it from him!"*

Final questions

? How do you suppose Elizabeth feels when John begins to confess?

? Was John right to accept death rather than make a false confession?

? Imagine yourself in the place of John or Elizabeth in this last scene. What would you have done?

? Draw a Mind Map or diagram of the various stages of "Proctor's Progress." Show how John moves from detachment to social involvement and on to his decision that he must die. Tag to the images on your drawing exact references to act and page number. You will find this useful when practicing essay questions or reviewing for your exam.

? The Salem "witches" were brutally tortured while in jail, but apart from the description of Giles's death, Miller hardly mentions this aspect. Why do you think he says so little about it? Would it have strengthened his play if he had put more emphasis on the physical sufferings of the victims?

well done! You've made it to the end!

GILES'S COUNTDOWN

1 Talks about his wife to Reverend Hale.
2 Confronts Judge Danforth.
3 Accuses Thomas Putnam.
4 Refuses to name informant.
5 Refuses to plead guilty or not guilty.

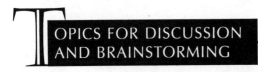

TOPICS FOR DISCUSSION AND BRAINSTORMING

One of the best ways to review is with one or more friends. Even if you're with someone who hardly knows the text you're studying, you'll find that having to explain things to your friend will help you to organize your own thoughts and memorize key points. If you're with someone who has studied the text, you'll find that the things you can't remember are different from the things your friend can't remember, so you'll help each other.

Discussion will also help you to develop interesting new ideas that perhaps neither of you would have had alone. Use a **brainstorming** approach to tackle any of the topics listed below. Allow yourself to share whatever ideas come into your head— however meaningless they seem. They will get you thinking creatively.

Whether alone or with a friend, use Mind Mapping (see p. vi) to help you brainstorm and organize your ideas. If you are with a friend, use a large sheet of paper and colored pens.

Any of the topics below could appear on an exam, but even if you think you've found one in your actual exam, be sure to answer the precise question given.

TOPICS

1 Why is this play called *The Crucible*?
2 Examine the way that the relationship between John and Elizabeth Proctor changes during the course of the play.
3 How much does Abigail Williams deserve our sympathy, and why?
4 Was Elizabeth right not to influence John's final decision? Why?
5 Choose two incidents from *The Crucible* and discuss how effectively they are presented in terms of dramatic structure and language.
6 Choose one of the main themes of *The Crucible* and show how Miller develops it thoughout the play.
7 What part do any two of the following play in *The Crucible*: Thomas Putnam, Giles Corey, Mary Warren, John Hale, Rebecca Nurse?
8 Reread the section How Historically Accurate Is *The Crucible*? (p. 5). Explain how Miller's changes make his play more exciting and effective, discussing at least three of the changes mentioned.

HOW TO GET AN "A" IN ENGLISH LITERATURE

In all your study, in coursework, and in exams, be aware of the following:

- **Characterization**—the characters and how we know about them (what they say and do, how the author describes them), their relationships, and how they develop.
- **Plot and structure**—what happens and how the plot is organized into parts or episodes.
- **Setting and atmosphere**—the changing scene and how it reflects the story (for example, a rugged landscape and storm reflecting a character's emotional problems).
- **Style and language**—the author's choice of words, and literary devices such as imagery, and how these reflect the mood.
- **Viewpoint**—how the story is told (for example, through an imaginary narrator, or in the third person but through the eyes of one character—"She was furious—how dare he!").
- **Social and historical context**—influences on the author (see Background in this book).

Develop your ability to:

- Relate **detail** to **broader content, meaning, and style.**
- Show understanding of the author's **intentions, technique, and meaning** (brief and appropriate comparisons with other works by the same author will earn credit).
- Give a **personal response and interpretation,** backed up by **examples** and short **quotations.**
- **Evaluate** the author's achievement (how far does the author succeed and why?).

Make sure you:

- Know how to use **paragraphs** correctly.
- Use a wide range of **vocabulary** and sentence structure.
- Use short, appropriate quotations as **evidence** of your understanding of that part of the text.
- Use **literary terms** to show your understanding of what the author is trying to achieve with language.

THE EXAM ESSAY

PLANNING

A literary essay of about 250 to 400 words on a theme from *The Crucible* will challenge your skills as an essay writer. it is worth taking some time to plan your essay carefully. An excellent way to do this is in the three stages below:

1 Make a **Mind Map** of your ideas on the theme suggested. Brainstorm and write down any ideas that pop into your head.
2 Taking ideas from your Mind Map, **organize** them into an outline choosing a logical sequence of information. Choose significant details and quotations to support your main thesis.
3 Be sure you have both a strong **opening paragraph** stating your main idea and giving the title and author of the literary work you will be discussing, and a **conclusion** that sums up your main points.

Then write the essay, allowing five minutes at the end for checking relevance, spelling, grammar, and punctuation.

WRITING AND EDITING

Write your essay carefully, allowing at least five minutes at the end to check for errors of fact as well as for correct spelling, grammar, and punctuation.
REMEMBER!
Stick to the thesis you are trying to support and avoid unnecessary plot summary. Always support your ideas with relevant details and quotations from the text.

*M*odel answer and plan

The next (and final) chapter consists of a model essay on a theme from *The Crucible*, followed by a Mind Map and an essay plan used to write it. Use these to get an idea of how an essay about *The Crucible* might be organized and how to break up your information into a logical sequence of paragraphs.

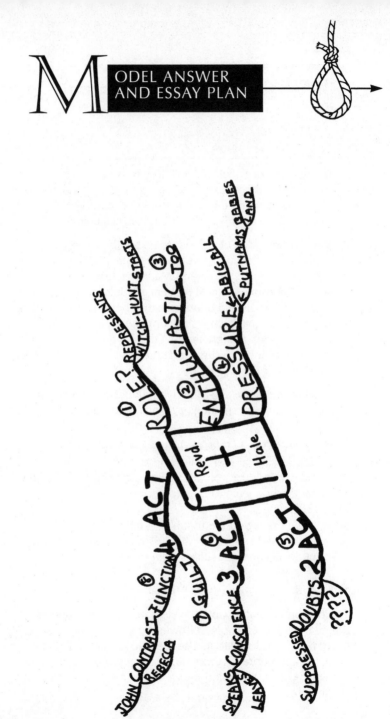

ACT 1

① ROLE? REPRESENTS

WITCH-HUNT STARTS

② ENTHUSIASTIC TOO

③

④ PRESSURE-ABIGAIL

& PUTNAMS RABIES AND

Revd. Hale

⑥ JOHN CONTRAST FUNCTION
REBECCA

ACT 3

⑦ GUILT

⑧ SPEAKS CONSCIENCE 3 ACT
LEAVES

⑤ SUPPRESSED DOUBTS 2 ACT
???

QUESTION

What is the role of Reverend Hale in the play?

PLAN

1 Who he is – his general function. Why Mr. Hale fits this role.
2 How he approaches his task in Act 1.
3 His downfall due to: (a) own character; (b) external circumstances.
4 Growing doubts in Act 2; absolute dissent in Act 3.
5 Act 4, inability to bear his guilt.
6 Function in the last act in contrast to John Proctor and Rebecca.

ESSAY

Reverend John Hale is a young minister from Beverly who appears in all four acts of *The Crucible*. His function changes with each act. In general, he stands for educated, intelligent people who allow themselves to be drawn into any kind of witch-hunt and then realize, too late, that they should have tried to prevent it.[1] Arthur Miller needs someone in authority with direct responsibility for setting off the series of events. He cannot bring in the judges at this early point in the play, so the role falls to Mr. Hale.[2]

In Act 1, Mr. Hale is full of pride at being summoned to give his expert opinion on Betty Parris's illness. He has brought along a stack of learned books "weighted with authority" to help him work this out. If left alone to do his work, Mr. Hale might never have decided there was witchcraft. We know he doesn't accept all the accusations laid before him, because Mr. Parris told Ann Putnam that one of Mr. Hale's previous cases turned out to be a false alarm.[3]

Unfortunately, Mr. Hale is very eager, and puts on a performance in front of Mr. and Mrs. Putnam and Abigail Williams. All three have some reason for wanting a positive result. Mrs. Putnam is looking for the killer of her dead babies, Mr. Putnam is probably already planning to get hold of his neighbors' farms, and Abigail needs to divert attention from her adventure in the forest.[4] When his Latin exorcism doesn't work, Mr. Hale begins to question Abigail: "Did you call the

Devil last night?" She immediately puts the blame on Mr. Parris's West Indian slave, Tituba. Mr. Hale forgets his first cautious approach and hardly notices that the Putnams are egging him on. By the end of Act 1, everyone except Tituba and the two girls is absolutely convinced that there are witches in Salem.[5]

In Act 2, Mr. Hale goes around to the farms to question people about their Christian faith. He is visiting the Proctors' house when news arrives that Rebecca and Martha have been arrested. Almost immediately, the court officials enter to take Elizabeth to jail. Hale tries desperately to justify her arrest to John, and to stifle a nagging doubt: "Proctor, the court is just." In Act 3, a long trial scene, Mr. Hale is unable to suppress what his conscience and common sense are telling him. He speaks up against the judges' corrupt procedures, but they brush aside his complaints: "I beg you, stop now before another is condemned! ... Private vengeance is working through this testimony!" Mr. Hale walks out of the court.[6]

The next time he appears (Act 4) is on the morning of the executions. Mr. Hale is a broken man. He knows he is more responsible than anyone for the deaths of the so-called witches. All he can do to soothe his conscience is to beg the remaining prisoners to lie and save their lives. At the end of the play, Mr. Hale's pitiful, guilty figure[7] accentuates the calm pride of John Proctor and Rebecca as they go out to meet their death on the gallows.[8]

WHAT'S SO GOOD ABOUT THIS ESSAY?

1 Clear identification of what the question is about.
2 Comment on structure of play.
3 Accurate recall of narrative plus one small but relevant detail.
4 Good grasp of characters' motivation.
5 Short but accurate summary of how the witch-hunt begins.
6 Again, accurate summary of narrative.
7 Evidence of personal response to the character.
8 Moving back from an outline of *events* to identification of his *function*—this is what the question is about.

GLOSSARY OF LITERARY TERMS

allegory an extended description of one thing in the form of another. Bunyan's *The Pilgrim's Progress*, the story of a journey, is really about the progress of the human soul. *The Crucible* began as an allegory for McCarthyism.

alliteration repetition of a sound at the beginnings of words, such as *ladies' lips.*

context the social and historical influences on the author.

dramatic irony where the audience knows something not known by one, or some, of the characters; for instance, when Elizabeth is asked if John is a lecher.

foreshadowing an indirect warning of things to come, often through imagery.

image a word picture used to make an idea come alive; for example, a **metaphor, simile,** or **personification** (see separate entries).

imagery the kind of word picture used to make an idea come alive.

irony (1) where the author or a character says the opposite of what they really think, or pretends ignorance of the true facts, usually for the sake of humor or ridicule; (2) where events turn out in what seems a particularly inappropriate way, as if mocking human effort.

metaphor description of a thing as if it were something essentially different, but also in some way similar; for example, *This farm's a continent when you go foot by foot droppin' seeds in it.* Here the metaphor emphasizes the huge effort needed to cultivate the farm.

personification a description of something (such as fate) as if it were a person.

prose   language in which, unlike verse, there is no set number of syllables in a line, and no rhyming.

protagonist   a play's main character. *The Crucible*'s protagonist is John Proctor.

setting   the place in which the action occurs, usually affecting the atmosphere, such as the court.

simile   a comparison of two things that are different in most ways but similar in one important way, and usually containing the word "like": *Dancing like heathen in the forest.*

structure   how the plot is organized.

theme   an idea explored by an author; for example, mass hysteria.

viewpoint   how the story is told by the writer. Events can be seen through the eyes of one character, several, or none in particular. This applies more to fiction than drama.

NDEX